T0030332

BEFORE THE
PARADE

Copyright © 2019, Rebecca Rose

All rights reserved. No part of this book may be reproduced, stored in a retrieval system or transmitted in any form or by any means without the prior written permission from the publisher, or, in the case of photocopying or other reprographic copying, permission from Access Copyright, 1 Yonge Street, Suite 1900, Toronto, Ontario M5E 1E5.

Nimbus Publishing Limited
3660 Strawberry Hill Street, Halifax, NS, B3K 5A9
(902) 455-4286 nimbus.ca

Printed and bound in Canada

NB1417

Design: Jenn Embree
Editor: Angela Mombourquette
Cover design inspired by the 1995 *Atlantic Canada Pride Guide* cover by Chris Aucoin

Library and Archives Canada Cataloguing in Publication

Title: Before the parade : a history of Halifax's gay, lesbian, and bisexual communities, 1972-1984 / Rebecca Rose.
Names: Rose, Rebecca, 1984- author.
Description: Includes bibliographical references.
Identifiers: Canadiana (print) 20190169230 | Canadiana (ebook) 20190169257 | ISBN 9781771087827 (softcover) | ISBN 9781771087834 (HTML)
Subjects: LCSH: Sexual minorities—Nova Scotia—Halifax—History—20th century. | LCSH: Sexual minorities—Nova Scotia—Halifax—Social conditions—20th century. | LCSH: Gays—Nova Scotia—Halifax—History—20th century. | LCSH: Gays—Nova Scotia—Halifax—Social conditions—20th century. | LCSH: Lesbians—Nova Scotia—Halifax—History—20th century. | LCSH: Lesbians—Nova Scotia—Halifax—Social conditions—20th century. | LCSH: Bisexuals—Nova Scotia—Halifax—History—20th century. | LCSH: Bisexuals—Nova Scotia—Halifax—Social conditions—20th century. | LCSH: Gay rights—Nova Scotia—Halifax—History—20th century. | LCSH: Gay activists—Nova Scotia—Halifax—History—20th century.
Classification: LCC HQ73.3.C22 H357 2019 | DDC 306.7609716/22—dc23

Nimbus Publishing acknowledges the financial support for its publishing activities from the Government of Canada, the Canada Council for the Arts, and from the Province of Nova Scotia. We are pleased to work in partnership with the Province of Nova Scotia to develop and promote our creative industries for the benefit of all Nova Scotians.

BEFORE THE
PARADE

A History of Halifax's Gay,

Lesbian, and Bisexual

Communities

1972 ▼ 1984

REBECCA ROSE

NIMBUS
PUBLISHING
NIMBUS.CA

*To the gay, lesbian, bisexual, two-spirit, transgender, queer, intersex,
and asexual activists and community members who came before
and made our existence and this book possible.
To my family and to my love.*

CONTENTS

THE VOICES

Below are brief biographical sketches of some of the individuals featured in this book in the context of their lives during the 1970s and early '80s.

MEREDITH BELL – Reclaim the Night organizer and volunteer at Bryony House. Performed at women's coffee houses, including at Odin's Eye on Argyle Street. Created Women's Film Series at the Nova Scotia College of Art and Design (now NSCAD University). Taught Wen-Do.

WALTER BORDEN – Gay Africadian/Mi'kmaw activist, actor, and playwright. Civil rights activist with The Nova Scotia Project, Black United Front (BUF), and Black Inmates Association. GAE member and Turret regular.

NANCY (HAMILTON) BRISTER – One of the few women who frequented the first gay bar in the Green Lantern building, Club 777, in the early 1970s. Ran a lesbian drop-in at the Brenton Street Women's Centre. GAE member, Help Line and Gayline volunteer, member of APPLE (Atlantic Provinces Political Lesbians for Equality), and member of the Rumours Management Committee.

BRENDA REBECCA BRYAN – Involved in renovating and opening A Woman's Place—Forrest House. Lived in a housing co-op the members referred to as "Dyke Motor Inn." Involved in the peace movement and the United Spinsters, an affinity group committed to non-violent direct action. Founding member of feminist newspaper *Pandora*. Manager of Rumours and member of the Halifax Women's Housing Co-op.

TOM BURNS – GAE founding member; elected first chairman of the alliance in 1972. Owner of Halifax's first gay bookstore, The Alternate Book Shop.

ANDREA CURRIE – Elected national student president of the Student Christian Movement (SCM), 1982–83. Rumours women's night regular. Involved in the local peace movement and the United Spinsters, an affinity group committed to non-violent direct action. Member of a capella quartet Four the Moment. Member of the Métis nation; Sixties Scoop survivor.

JIM DEYOUNG – GAE founding member. Lived in an apartment in the Green Lantern building and in the Morris Street apartments.

ANNE FULTON – Founding member and first secretary of the GAE. One of the few women to frequent Club 777 in the early 1970s. Active within the GAE Civil Rights Committee; was elected GAE chairperson. Started autonomous lesbian group, the Atlantic Provinces Political Lesbians for Equality (APPLE); ran the Alliance's Gayline for a time.

REG GILES – Lived in the Green Lantern building and worked as security, maintenance, coat check, DJ, and bar staff at The Turret. Directed and performed in Turret variety shows; founding member and executive director of the Gay Artists Musicians and Entertainers Society (GAMES).

DAVID GRAY – Founding member and chairman of the GAE. Lived in the Green Lantern building and owned Club 777 and Thee Klub (AKA David's) gay bar.

DIANN GRAHAM – Worked for Women's Employment Outreach (WEO) located at A Woman's Place—Forrest House. Served on International Women's Day (IWD) and Reclaim the Night organizing committees. Member of the Halifax Women's Housing Co-op.

DIANE GUILBAULT – On the organizing committee for Reclaim the Night (also known as Take Back the Night) and worked at Bryony House women's shelter. On various organizing committees for International Women's Day. Briefly a member of APPLE.

SUSAN HOLMES – Single mother and member of the Anarcha-Feminist group that organized Reclaim the Night. Member of APPLE and the Work for Women Co-op. Founding member of the Halifax Women's Housing Co-op.

LORNE IZZARD – Gay Black man who moved to Halifax from Truro in 1974. Thee Klub regular and DJ at Condon's bar in the Green Lantern building; Turret regular. HIV/AIDS activist.

BARBARA JAMES – Feminist/socialist/anti-racist activist for sexuality and reproductive rights. Founding member of the Abortion Information and Referral Service (AIRS) in the late 1970s.

RANDY KENNEDY – GAE member; performed as drag queen Lily Champagne at The Turret and Rumours; founding member of the Gay Artists Musicians and Entertainers Society (GAMES). Staff at both The Turret and Rumours. Lived in the Morris Street apartments.

NAOMI LECHINSKY – Lesbian feminist activist; got involved with Women Against Violence Against Women (WAVAW) in the early 1980s. Founding member of the Halifax Women's Housing Co-op.

KATHERINE MACNEIL – Moved from Cape Breton to attend Mount Saint Vincent University. GAE executive member and Turret regular.

SCOTT MACNEIL – Regular at Thee Klub, Condon's, The Turret, and Rumours. Founding member of Halifax's first AIDS organization, the Gay Health Association.

JAMES MACSWAIN – Involved in the GAE's Civil Rights Committee. Cultural coordinator for the 1978 national gay and lesbian conference held in Halifax; cast member of *The Night They Raided Truxx*. Created and acted in *The Bearded Lady's Reflection* and co-curated Art By Gay Men with Robin Metcalfe.

MARY ANN MANCINI – One of the only women to frequent Thee Klub in the Green Lantern building; volunteered at The Turret; GAE member; involved in the Alliance's Speakers Bureau. Editor of the GAE's *The Voice of Canada's Ocean Playground*. Involved in Gay Alcoholics Anonymous.

ANITALOUISE MARTINEZ – Former resident, volunteer, and employee at Bryony House. Has been photographing 2SLGBTQIA+ and feminist events since 1984.

ANN MCMULLIN – Founding member of GAE; long-time partner of (fellow founding member) Diane Warren. Ann and Diane were one of the first lesbian couples to go to Club 777.

ROBIN METCALFE – Helped to revive the GAE in 1975 and launch *The Other Side* disco, which would become The Turret. GAE Secretary and chairperson, and member of the Alliance's Civil Rights Committee. Wrote for the *The Body Politic* and published and wrote for *Making Waves*. Co-curated Art By Gay Men with James MacSwain. Local 2SLGBTQIA+ archivist and historian.

CAROL MILLETT – Lesbian and anti-racist activist who was born and raised in north end Halifax. Member of socialist group In Struggle and involved in organizing International Women's Day. Taught Wen-Do and was a member of the Halifax Women's Housing Co-op.

LYNN MURPHY – Bisexual and feminist activist. Involved in A Woman's Place—Forrest House. Member of the GAE Civil Rights Committee and Speakers Bureau. Sat on the GAE executive as female-without-portfolio and chairperson.

SANDRA NIMMO – The first lesbian in Nova Scotia to gain full custody of her children. Staff person at A Woman's Place—Forrest House. Involved in creating, and later sat on the board for, Bryony House. Member of APPLE.

FAITH NOLAN – Activist and musician of mixed African, Mi'kmaw, and Irish heritage. Returned to Halifax from Toronto in 1976 at nineteen years old. Played guitar and sang at women's coffee houses and folk nights at The Turret.

CHRIS SHEPHERD – African Nova Scotian gay man from the Crichton Avenue Extension in Dartmouth. Regular at Thee Klub; DJ at The Turret. GAE treasurer who lived in the Morris Street apartments.

ANTHONY (TONY) TRASK – General member of GAE; served on GAE executive as secretary, and on Turret Management Committee (TMC). Coordinator of GAE Speakers Bureau and Gayline. Salaried correspondence secretary for GAE from 1979 to 1981. Turret regular and volunteer.

DEBORAH TRASK – Got involved in the GAE in 1976 and was one of three GAE members who signed the lease for The Turret's space. Served six terms on the GAE executive, including as chairperson in 1982.

DIANE WARREN – GAE founding member, later elected chairman. Help Line volunteer; pitched the idea of the Gayline. Long-time partner of fellow founding member, Ann McMullin. Ann and Diane were one of the first lesbian couples to go to Club 777.

DARL WOOD – Joined the military in 1975 and was discharged for having a relationship with a woman in 1978. GAE board member and Gayline volunteer. Spoke out publicly about the military's LGB purge throughout the 1980s. Lesbian feminist activist who was involved in Voice of Women. Part white, part Blackfoot, and part African-Canadian.

PREFACE

Though we never met, in many ways Anne Fulton is the reason I am writing this book.

Fulton, one of the foremothers of lesbian activism in Halifax, and a founding member of the Gay Alliance for Equality (GAE), passed away unexpectedly in November 2015. By the time I was organizing within the queer and trans community in Halifax, Fulton—who was more than thirty years my senior—had long since retreated from gay and lesbian activism.

It was Robin Metcalfe who told me about Anne's death at one of our regular coffee dates. A local activist, historian, archivist, and art gallery director and curator, Robin was my entry point into Halifax's—to use the vernacular of the day—gay and lesbian activist history.

Fittingly, Robin and I met in 2012 at Veith House where he was giving a presentation on the origins of our national gay holiday, Pink Triangle Day, for the current-day 2SLGBTQIA+ (two spirit, lesbian, gay, bisexual, transgender, queer, intersex, asexual, plus) advocacy group the Nova Scotia Rainbow Action Project (NSRAP). Ours was the first close relationship I developed with one of my "elders."

Robin and Anne had been a dynamic duo during the fevered days of gay liberation in the mid-1970s. Anne was active within the GAE Civil Rights Committee, attended national gay and lesbian conferences, started an autonomous lesbian group (APPLE), and ran the Alliance's Gayline for a time. She was also one of the few women to frequent one of Halifax's first gay bars, Club 777, in the early 1970s.

Three months after her death, Halifax's alternative weekly, *The Coast*, published my profile of Fulton—"Memories of a Founding Mother of Gay and

Lesbian Activism"—which, in part, lamented how little attention her passing had garnered from anyone outside her immediate circles. The story led me to search out other stories and write an expansive account of lesbian, gay, and bisexual life and activism in 1970s Halifax for *The Coast*'s 2016 Pride edition: the original "Before the Parade."

Previously, the most substantial published account of lesbian, gay, and bisexual organizing in Nova Scotia (to my knowledge) was Robin's essay in the catalogue for the "Queer Looking, Queer Acting" art exhibit, which he curated, at the Mount Saint Vincent University (MSVU) Art Gallery in 1997. In that essay, Robin charts local LGB activism through the examination of ephemera—flyers, posters, buttons, placards, and the like.

I first heard many of the names of the people in this book at the table in Robin's apartment in Halifax. Robin has an uncanny ability to recall people, places, and events. I imagine his mind, much like his apartment and his archives: meticulously organized, with memories ready to be plucked and dusted off at a moment's notice.

In lieu of an official 2SLGBTQIA+ archive, Robin's is surely the largest collection of gay, lesbian, bisexual, and queer archival documents and materials in the province. Thirty years my senior, Robin was (and still is) working to preserve local LGB history as it was unfolding: ensuring that the GAE sent copies of minutes to the Canadian Lesbian and Gay Archives (CLGA) and squirrelling away materials since he got involved in the mid-1970s. He has boxes upon boxes of archival materials at his home in Sheet Harbour, NS.

Fellow GAE alumni continue to send him bits and pieces in the mail for safekeeping. Anthony Trask is one of those people. "He's sort of the master archivist for everything," says Anthony, who was in charge of sending GAE materials to the CLGA. "Always was."

On more than one occasion Robin has let me root through the typewritten minutes, handwritten notes, flyers and posters, matchbooks, and other items that comprise his archives. After Anne passed, Robin inherited her personal collection, which he will one day entrust to a public archive.

Throughout the course of my research, I have been welcomed in to countless homes, offered tea and snacks, and spent time leafing through many personal archives and photo albums. I've been gifted with photocopies and even originals of newsletters, pamphlets, worn copies of gay and lesbian history

Robin Metcalfe and Anne Fulton perform at the talent show at The Turret during the 1977 Atlantic Gay Conference in Halifax. **(ROBIN METCALFE COLLECTION)**

books, and essay collections published in the '70s. Anthony Trask even gave me my very own yellow and blue "Gay Rights Now" button, which was produced by the National Gay Rights Coalition (NGRC) in 1976. I have been a messenger, delivering a "hello" or even long-ago borrowed books between friends who have fallen out of touch. Often I have been the one to tell people who is still alive and who is dead.

I have also spent a great deal of time in the Nova Scotia Archives poring through files from the early days of the GAE. I often wonder if I am the only person retrieving these files, combing through the typewritten (and sometimes handwritten) minutes from general and executive meetings, looking for hints of what it was like to be gay, lesbian, bi, queer, or two-spirit in 1970s and '80s Halifax.

By way of my research and writing, I have been on the receiving end of countless stories of gay, lesbian, bisexual, and two-spirit life back home in Nova Scotia, back then.

This book is an attempt to make sure those histories don't end up only in my head, on my computer, in my personal archives.

▼

This keen interest in the past is not a new thing for me. My sense of self is and always has been firmly rooted in, well, my roots.

Growing up I spent summers at my family's cottage in Cape Breton (Unama'ki), nestled between the woods and the ocean, where my mother's family has resided since the 1800s. I have always revelled in family folklore and have maintained strong relationships with my older family members.

My mother is the record-keeper in her family; in our living room sits a chest filled with scraps of paper scrawled with my grandmother's handwriting, and with black and white pictures sorted meticulously and filed in binders. It also holds my great-grandmother's journals and a large handwritten family tree reaching back to the 1700s. I inherited both my mother's curiosity and her desire to document it all.

I was seventeen years old when I first came out as bisexual to my close friends. Months later I moved from Dartmouth to Toronto to study journalism at Ryerson University, located just blocks away from Toronto's gay village.

Like most newly minted queers, I set out to find "my people." Searching for and building queer and trans community has been a through-line of my adult life.

As Deborah Trask said of her many years involved in the GAE, our community is made of people "who have nothing in common but their difference from societal norms," so we don't usually grow up with our elders, hearing stories of 2SLGBTQIA+ life and activism gone by. Our histories don't often appear in textbooks and curricula.

It is not until much later that we learn about our collective beginnings: the police brutality and riotous protests that birthed the modern day North American gay rights movement, and eventually Pride celebrations, in California, New York, and beyond; the trans women, lesbians, gay men, queens, sex workers, and street youth who fought back.

As a queer femme, I first located *my* history in the pages of Leslie Feinberg's 1993 novel *Stone Butch Blues*. This first-person exploration of life as a working-class stone butch (a very masculine lesbian) was my window into 1960s butch/femme bar culture and my introduction to the unapologetically feminine queer women—often sex workers—who came before me.

In the 1970s it was a "revelation" for Robin to learn about Germany's homosexual emancipation movement: the Scientific-Humanitarian Committee, founded in 1897, and Berlin's Institute for Sexual Research, founded in 1919. The Institute conducted research and provided education on sex and sexuality, as well as counselling, electrolysis, and gender confirming surgery, to homosexual, transgender, and intersex people. It advocated for the decriminalization of homosexual acts, for the right of intersex people to choose their sex at age eighteen, and successfully pressured the police to issue licenses allowing trans people to move freely throughout Berlin.

On May 6, 1933, Nazis burned thousands of books, photographs, and other materials considered "un-German" belonging to the Institute in Berlin's Opera Square.

"Part of the 'never again' that comes of the Holocaust—we never again want to forget our history," Robin told me in 2016. "There are many ways that it can be forgotten or erased, other than the brute repression of the Nazis."

For a group that has focused so heavily on making itself visible (though this is not everyone's goal, I know), being made invisible—whether as a result of colonization and genocide, a concerted political campaign, an epidemic, or just plain ignorance—is a blow.

I began writing this book not long after Doug Ford's Progressive Conservative government removed gender identity, same-sex relationships, and consent from the province's elementary school curriculum. In addition to repealing the sex-ed curriculum, the Ford government cancelled a series of Truth and Reconciliation writing sessions aimed at integrating First Nations history and perspectives into the curriculum. In September 2018 my girlfriend and I sat in awe, faces soaked in happy tears, as forty thousand high school students walked out of school in protest of these changes.

In October of that same year the *New York Times* reported that the Trump administration was considering a law that would define gender and sex as binary, determined by one's genitals, and immovable—effectively denying the existence of transgender, non-binary, and intersex people. The outcry was summed up with the popular hashtag #wewontbeerased.

Only a month later, the membership of the Ontario Progressive Conservatives passed a resolution calling "gender identity theory" a "highly controversial, unscientific, 'liberal ideology'" that ought not be taught in Ontario schools.

These recent attacks have made me even more passionate about making sure that our communities' stories are preserved, and most importantly, shared.

As butch and trans icon Leslie Feinberg wrote in the afterword for the tenth anniversary edition of *Stone Butch Blues*: "Recovering collective memory is in itself an act of struggle."

INTRODUCTION

"We recognize the importance of making known our history, so much of which has been lost or stolen."

RESOLUTION PASSED AT THE 1979 MEETING OF THE
CANADIAN LESBIAN AND GAY RIGHTS COALITION

This is the beginning of the motion that established February 14 as Pink Triangle Day, our national gay holiday. The resolution has a distinctly Nova Scotia connection, having been proposed by the Gay Alliance for Equity (GAE), Nova Scotia's first gay and lesbian advocacy group, and penned by well-known Nova Scotian gay activist elder Robin Metcalfe.

And that is what this book is about: making known the history of the lesbian, gay, and bisexual community and activism in Halifax; of this province's first generation of out and activist 2SLGB elders.

It is a history of people finding each other in unlicensed gay clubs, in church basements, while cruising the sidewalks of "The Triangle," and at house parties. It is one of taking up space and creating our own spaces: a lesbian drop-in at a women's centre; a community–run bar-cum-drop-in-centre; a gay bookstore; a women's housing co-op. One of playing with gender; of drag queens; of women in button-down shirts and workboots; and of lots of disco and lots of sex. A history of gay men and women sometimes working together and sometimes not; of bisexual women and lesbian mothers trying to find their place within lesbian separatist politics; of Black LGBTQ folks navigating mostly white spaces and making their own.

It is one of being at the forefront: of founding a group to fight for gay liberation just three years after the Stonewall riots; of initiating the first nationally coordinated gay and lesbian day of action in 1977; of producing the first national lesbian newsletter that same year; and of hosting a national gay and lesbian conference in 1978. Our activist history is woven from a gay phone line, a campaign to include sexual orientation in the Human Rights Act twenty years before it finally was, pickets at bars, boycotts of the CBC, guerrilla feminist actions, Reclaim the Night, and more.

It is a history that has shaped not only the 2SLGBTQIA+ (two-spirit, lesbian, gay, bisexual, transgender, queer, intersex, asexual, plus) community in Halifax, but Halifax and Nova Scotia as a whole, in ways that many may not know. It is also one that is not always given its due. I have skimmed many a Canadian LGB history book that claims to be national in scope, only to find little to no Nova Scotian content; our contributions have been left off timelines of important dates in 2SLGBTQIA+ history; and I am always surprised by how many people I meet outside of the Maritime provinces who know nothing of Nova Scotia's rich 2SLGBTQIA+ history.

THE PINK TRIANGLE

Pink Triangle Day was named to mark the (first) acquittal of the officers of Pink Triangle Press, which published *The Body Politic*, the national gay paper of record printed in Toronto in the 1970s and '80s. In 1978 Pink Triangle Press and its officers were charged with "possession of obscene material for distribution" and "use of the mails to distribute immoral, indecent and scurrilous materials."

Throughout the Holocaust, queers were interned in concentration camps alongside Jewish and Roma people, communists, union activists, and Jehovah's Witnesses. In the camps, gay men were made to wear pink triangles on the left side of their jackets or on the right leg of their pants. The pink triangle has since been reclaimed—much like the word queer—by some as a symbol of pride, a more politically charged rainbow flag. The black triangle, given to lesbians in the camps, is now a lesser-known symbol of LGB liberation.

▼

In 2013, I was on the Board for the Nova Scotia Rainbow Action Project (NSRAP) and in charge of decorating for our annual fundraising gala. For our celebration of queer and trans activism, past and present, we plastered the walls of a hotel ballroom with posters, many of which NSRAP staffer Chris Aucoin had photocopied from Robin's archives. It was a tactile timeline of sorts: it included a copy of the original Turret logo (Wite-Out and all); posters for the 1970s lefty bookstore Red Herring Cooperative Books, and for The Turret's successor, Rumours, for International Women's Day marches, and for the 1990s Black gay and lesbian social group JUKA. The timeline continued right up to the "queer and rebel days" and the "dyke and trans march" of the early 2000s.

NSRAP was not alone in paying homage to local 2SLGBTQIA+ activist history during the aughts.

I have witnessed an influx of queer and trans activists, disillusioned by a movement that felt like it stalled with the introduction of same-sex marriage and Pride celebrations, who have drawn inspiration from our activist roots.

Over the past decade, activists of all ages have made a series of overtures to preserve and promote our history: an intentionally intergenerational camp-out at the lesbian-owned Mermaid and the Cow campground in Pictou County; the Lesbian Memory Keepers workshop, which brought lesbian and bisexual women together to document their history in 2004; a 1970s-style cabaret and disco paying tribute to The Turret held by the NSCAD Queer Collective in the old Khyber building; Robin's remounting of the *Queer Looking, Queer Acting* art exhibit; a bevy of panels on our LGBTQ history; and an old-fashioned salon where elders shared their stories—the first of which was held in July 2018—organized by the Elderberries, a group of LGBTQ people over fifty.

And there have been efforts to get much of it into print and on film: a series of essays in the *OUT: Queer Looking, Queer Acting* catalogue; Dan MacKay's GayHalifax wiki page, a collaboratively edited website where community members document local history; Chris Aucoin's Halifax Pride thirtieth-anniversary souvenir magazine which documents the history of the festival; the "We Dreamed Another Way of Being" Lesbian Memory Keepers report; NSRAP's youth and elders video project where queer and trans youth interview LGBT elders; as well as Reg Giles's *Peanut Butter and Jam Sandwich (THRU MY EYES)* and Scott MacNeil's *Reflections In A Mirror Ball,* both accounts of gay (night) life in Halifax in the 1970s and '80s published on Gay Halifax. These are just a few that I know of.

All of this, and more, has been my personal map to uncovering this particular corner (corners, really) of the past.

▼

As I wrote in an article titled "Before the Parade" in *The Coast* in 2016, "these conversations, these relationships—the first between young activists and those 30, 40 and even 50 years our seniors—are in themselves historic."

There have always been people whom we might today call two-spirit, gay, lesbian, bisexual, transgender, or queer. In many cultures, heterosexuality, monogamy, and the gender binary are fairly new concepts, often forced upon them by colonization and religion.

There was, however, no visible lesbian, gay, and bisexual activist movement in Halifax prior to the early 1970s, so the activists I talked to for this book didn't have out and activist elders to look to.

In 1970s and '80s Halifax there were older LGB folks who were out to a certain degree, who had connected with each other at things like dinner and house parties, cruising, and at the club. Carol Millet, a lesbian and anti-racist activist who was born and raised in north end Halifax, says that for her the folks from the generation before hers were the "real trailblazers, even though they weren't out in the way that we know it now."

But the very thing that acts as a bridge between me and my elders—our passion for 2SLGBTQIA+ activism—was what alienated some of the people of Robin Metcalfe's generation from their elders, Robin tells me.

"Our activism was a barrier between us and older gays," he says.

As a queer in my thirties, it has been affirming to get to know my elders—2SLGBQ people in their sixties, seventies, and eighties—through the researching and writing of this book.

We often hear about how representation (in the media, in entertainment, in literature) matters for those who inhabit marginalized identities. And it does. Beyond that, a wide variety of representation matters. As 2SLGBTQIA+

folks, it is important that what we read, what we watch, what we listen to reflects our layered identities: a variety of sexualities and gender expressions, a range of racial identities, different classes, differing abilities, a plethora of lived experiences. I think, too, we need to see, watch, and listen to people of all different ages.

Queer culture—like the wider culture in which it resides—can have a tendency to worship youth, and North American Pride celebrations often embody these attitudes. The young, commonly skinny but "ripped," men who dance atop floats and the countless late-night dance parties (where, as a queer in my thirties, I have sometimes been one of the older folks in the room).

Nancy Brister came out as a lesbian in Halifax in the early 1970s, following a difficult divorce from the father of her son. One of the few women who frequented the first gay bar in the Green Lantern building—Club 777—Nancy also ran a lesbian drop-in at the Brenton Street Women's Centre. Sitting across the table from me at the Glitter Bean Café, Nancy—now in her late seventies—talks about the feeling of invisibility that can accompany aging. "Once we're a certain age, we're not part of life anymore," she says. "Suddenly your opinion doesn't matter." For 2SLGBTQIA+ elders, that invisibility can be two-pronged. "Because anybody over fifty everyone assumes is straight," Nancy muses.

I often witness people around me infantilize people over a "certain age." Seniors are automatically "adorable, sweet, precious"—regardless of their demeanour. Some parts of mainstream North American society also struggle with the idea that people over sixty—save some notable "older" men still deemed to be hunks in Hollywood—can be sexual beings.

All of this means that we, as a society, may overlook the fact that these elders are the ones who changed our perceptions of sex, sexuality, and gender; who fought for and won many of the gains we benefit from today.

For younger queers and trans folks, getting to know our elders demonstrates that we can, in fact, grow older. There are many reasons that 2SLGBTQIA+ people may not envision making it to our sixties or beyond. I personally have known two people killed by homophobic violence, one in Toronto and one in Halifax, while other friends have survived horrendous attacks. Each year dozens of trans people are murdered, precisely because they are trans, and young trans women of colour that I know express surprise that they are still alive. News of the members of the 2SLGBTQIA+ communities in both Canada and the United States (including in Nova Scotia) who have taken their own lives dot my Facebook newsfeed.

Elders also demonstrate what we are capable of—not in spite of our queerness and/or trans-ness, but because of it. The elders I spoke to for this book have lived full lives; the type of gay, lesbian, or queer lives that are (still) not always portrayed onscreen, in books, or in mainstream media. The types of lives that some of us were told—by our families of origin, our places of worship, our peers—that we wouldn't be able to have. They have experienced success, known heartbreak, created vital 2SLGBTQIA+ spaces, immersed themselves in LGB, feminist, anti-racist, and peace activism and have pulled back in order to live quieter lives (often only to re-engage later on). They have fostered chosen families.

"Oh, I loved my life," Nancy tells me when I ask her about how she looks back on those early days. She has recently reconnected with other 2SLGBTQIA+ elders—her community—through the Elderberries. "It's just great being with them," she says.

I often wonder if young 2SLGBTQIA+ folks actually think of themselves as "in community" with 2SLGBTQIA+ people over sixty, or if we/they view our elders as belonging firmly to the communities of the past. I personally believe that, in order to address some of the schisms that exist in our community—over corporate and police participation in Pride festivals, trans-inclusive spaces, and even the language we use to describe ourselves and other members of the community—we will need to come together across generations and do the work of trying to understand just where we're all coming from.

While I was writing this book, Mary Ann Mancini died. I never met Mary Ann face to face; the first time we spoke over the phone was for the profile I was writing about Anne Fulton. Though Mary Ann did not want to be interviewed for the larger article in *The Coast* (for personal reasons), we kept in touch via Facebook Messenger. We talked about her COPD and her move to Northwood, a continuing care residence in Halifax. She sent me pictures of how she wanted to embellish her wheelchair (there were plenty of rainbows). She expressed her frustration that she wasn't able to enjoy the fruits of her labour by attending the Pride parade; she told me to take lots of pictures. Next year, she joked, maybe powerchairs could lead the Pride parade, as the Dykes on Bikes do for the Dyke March each year in Toronto. She told me about a trans child she knew who was struggling at school; it weighed heavily on her heart. We discussed our divergent views on Halifax Pride. I don't know what impact, if any, these conversations had on Mary Ann, but our back-and-forth made an indelible mark on me. I hope that, like my conversations with Mary Ann, this book can play a role in bringing together community members from various generations.

In her last message, in December 2018, Mary Ann told me she was sick with pneumonia. Mary Ann's death was an unwelcome reminder that our elders, and the histories they keep, won't be around forever.

▼

There is no one history of gay, lesbian, and bisexual community and activism in Halifax or in Nova Scotia. This is a collection of stories and insights from some of the people who—by way of living their lives, and their activism—made it possible for so many of us to exist, to be out, to be proud, to continue to push for change.

In large part, this book focuses on lesbian, gay, and bisexual activism in the 1970s and early '80s in the most commonly understood sense of the word: outward political advocacy. We know, though, that activism is broader than that.

As Nancy Brister told me during our first telephone conversation in 2016: "If you come out, that's political, even if you don't do another thing. I've carried banners, too. But I think just being counted is political." For 2SLGBTQIA+ folks—today and forty years ago—existing, surviving, and thriving in this world is political, is its own kind of activism. Central to Nova Scotia's LGB history is Nova Scotia's Gay Alliance for Equality (GAE), which was founded by a group of working-class women and men in 1972.

When I started writing about this history—these histories—my primary focus was on the activities of the GAE, as it was the province's only official gay and lesbian advocacy group during the 1970s and early 1980s. And while GAE was (and is) central, there were other groups, other physical spaces where LGB2S people—specifically those who were not white or male—found community.

"For most women I know, lesbian activism was a part of the wider women's movement," Halifax-raised LGB and feminist activist Barbara James writes in an email. "I came to activism through an interest in human rights and reproductive rights before there was much of a visible gay/lesbian rights movement, at least in Halifax."

One of the things this book explores in detail is the women's and peace groups where many L, B, and 2S women found their people and honed their activism.

"All these little bits make a movement," Carol Millet says, of the various actions she attended in the 1970s and '80s. "They really weren't little at all." In 2014 Robin Metcalfe re-mounted the *Queer Looking, Queer Acting* exhibit, this time at the interim Khyber Centre for the Arts space in north end Halifax. The Khyber reprinted the 1997 catalogue—including Robin's groundbreaking essay "Queer Looking, Queer Acting, Seeks Same," as well as essays from writer and activist Jane Kansas and Jim MacSwain—and added new essays from Robin, me, independent curator and writer Genevieve Flavelle, and transmedia artist Beck Gilmer-Osborne.

In my *OUT: Queer Looking, Queer Acting Revisited* essay, entitled "Beyond Lesbian and Gay," I wrote: "What struck me most when first reading Robin Metcalfe's essay in the original *Queer Looking, Queer Acting* catalogue was the continuous use of 'gay and lesbian.' Gay and lesbian, gay and lesbian, gay and lesbian. ('Queer' snuck in there in the 1990s.) Gay and lesbian, or even simply 'queer,' is not reflective of the community or movement that I have been immersed in over the past five years."

You may feel the same way reading this book. Language changes, and in the 2SLGBTQIA+ community, language can change very quickly. When it comes to people who are not heterosexual, the language has changed fairly recently from "homophile" to "homosexual," to "gay and lesbian," to "gay, lesbian, and bisexual," to "queer." Many people that I have interviewed do not like or use the word "queer" to describe themselves. Throughout this book I have tried to use the language that folks were using at the time, which is why in many cases I have trimmed the acronym down to LGB. (As I'll discuss, many "L" and "G" people and communities have not, and still do not, always include or accept our "B" community members.)

It also means I am not, necessarily, documenting trans history. Transgender, gender non-conforming, and gender variant people have always existed—this I know. Like the language used to describe LGB people, the language has changed and continues to change. How people understand gender, gender identity, the gender spectrum, and gender fluidity, is also (thankfully) ever-changing. While conducting interviews for this book I have been told of several people who may have identified as transgender women today—who took hormones or had what we now call gender-confirming surgery. Many of these folks are also African-Nova Scotian. Some of these people have passed away; some are alive but no longer live in Halifax; folks have fallen out of contact. I am aware that some people have likely changed their names and it is not clear if those who are alive are "out" as being transgender, or if they want to be found. I would have liked to include some of those stories in this book. The community I am a part of, and the activism I engage in, is distinctly queer and trans, trans and queer—and that is the history I am interested in and passionate about.

This book is also the result of countless hours spent in various archives. I am under no illusion, though, that archives—any archives—can fully capture our collective histories. The archives that I spend my time in contain primarily minutes of meetings, communiqués, newsletters, newspaper clippings, posters, flyers—and in the case of personal archives, photographs. I often reflect upon who feels safe, able, and empowered enough to document their lives in these ways, and then to hand these things over to an institution (in the case of public archives) that may not have always been accepting of them and their community. Monica Forrester, a two-spirit, Black, trans and queer femme sex worker and activist living in Toronto, wrote in *Marvellous Grounds: Queer of Colour Histories of Toronto*: "And when I was thinking about history and archiving, I thought, 'Oh! I wish I took pictures.' Because we were in such a different place back then. I think survival was key. No one really thought about archiving, because we really didn't think we would live past 30. Our lives were so undetermined that no one really thought about, 'Oh should we archive this for later use?'"

My intention from the very beginning of this project has been to feature the stories of Mi'kmaw 2SLGB people. Mi'kmaw people have been living on Mi'kma'ki for over thirteen thousand years. Theirs is the territory that Nova Scotia inhabits, and on which I researched and wrote large parts of this book. My application to Mi'kmaw Ethics Watch at Unama'ki College, however, coincided with internal restructuring, which delayed my approval. As such, the folks with Mi'kmaw heritage who I was able to interview were people with whom I had already made contact or developed a relationship. I thank Mi'kmaw Ethics Watch for the important work that they do and encourage other writers and editors to familiarize themselves with the MEW process.

I hope that what I have been able to collect here serves as a catalyst for the further exploration and telling of 2SLGBTQIA+ histories that remain untold or under-told.

▼

Documenting history thirty, forty, or even fifty years down the road can be challenging: people's memories fade; they remember things differently; remembrances become stories, become folklore.

As Deborah Trask often reminds me: "The past is a foreign country: they do things differently there." (A quote from L. P. Hartley's novel *The Go-Between.*)

And it's true, no matter how much I read, how many elders I talk to, I will never fully understand what it was like to be gay, lesbian, bisexual, or two-spirit in Halifax back when homosexuality and bisexuality were just emerging from our collective closet. The events outlined in this book are only snippets of people's lives, of a time and place. I have tried my best to put the events herein into context in relation to the broader Canadian and North American homophile and gay and lesbian liberation movements, and in relation to the civil rights and Black power movements, the struggles of First Nations people in this country, the women's movement, and the peace movement. I have also included glimpses what was happening terms of big-P politics, legal wrangling, art, music, and more.

I feel a huge sense of responsibility holding, and now retelling, these stories, as they are not mine. In fact, I was not alive for most of them. I've chosen to end this book the year I was born: 1984.

But that is not the only reason. Many of the elders I have spoken to draw an invisible line through their recollections: pre- and post-AIDS and AIDS activism. The movement and its aims, the community, the people, all changed after HIV/AIDS came to the fore. The community's response to the crisis in the 1980s, 1990s, and beyond also deserves special attention. There is simply too much to fit into the pages of this book. (The AIDS Activist

History Project has posted over a dozen interviews with Nova Scotian AIDS activists on its website.)

I hope to never know what it's like to live through something like the AIDS epidemic in North America; I have a great deal of respect for those who do know. The outbreak robbed the community of so many beautiful, brilliant, creative, loving, and loved individuals. We will never know what our community, the movement, would have looked like, would have accomplished, if it hadn't. It also took from us large chunks of our collective memory.

Bisexual activist elder Lynn Murphy lived through the crisis, and knows the importance of documenting, and keeping safe, these stories.

"People are aware that people get old and die," she tells me from the recliner in her downtown Halifax apartment. "And in the worst of the AIDS crisis they weren't getting very old when they died. Who would care about this stuff after we were gone? We [are] made invisible."

▼

Not far from Lynn's apartment is the Glitter Bean Café. The explicitly queer-and-trans unionized co-op café was opened in spring 2018 by former baristas at the Smiling Goat Organic Espresso Bar after the owner abruptly closed several locations.

While I was home during the sweltering summer of that year, I conducted interviews and wrote from the delightfully gay café. The first time I set foot inside the turquoise, pink, gold, and glittery walls of the aptly named Glitter Bean, I cried happy tears.

In the back room of the café a timeline of local queer and trans businesses was tacked to a giant corkboard just above a library of donated 2SLGBTQIA+ books. During one of my meetings with Black gay elder Lorne Izzard, we stood together in front of the timeline, reading about one of the first gay bars in Halifax, Thee Klub in the Green Lantern building, and the GAE-run Turret club and de facto community centre, among others; places that Lorne would soon bring to life during our interview. Lorne grew up in Amherst and moved to Halifax from Truro in 1974. There we were, a gay Black man of sixty-five and a queer white woman of thirty-three communing over our shared history.

Chapter 1

SAFE SPACES, SUBVERSIVE SEX

(Late 1960s and Early 1970s)

1969 was an eventful year for 2SLGBTQIA+ folks in North America.

In the late days of June of that year, the patrons of the Stonewall Inn, a New York City hangout for gays, lesbians, drag queens, transgender people, street youth, and sex workers, fought back against repeated police raids and abuse. Hundreds took part in the riotous protests—including the now-iconic Marsha P. Johnson, Miss Major Griffin-Gracy, Stormé DeLarverie, and Sylvia Rivera—and on that first night, thirteen were arrested. On June 29—in a city often credited as a birthplace of gay liberation in North America—the headline of a *New York Times* article about the riots read: "4 Policemen Hurt in 'Village' Raid."

That same day, a teenaged Anne Fulton graduated from high school in New Brunswick, according to a handwritten account found amongst her papers and keepsakes.

"On the day of the Stonewall Riots, I marched to the front of my high school auditorium in my little white dress to the strains of 'Land of Hope and Glory' and was presented with my graduation certificate," Anne wrote. "While drag queens in New York were rebelling in the streets in their finest chiffon, there I was being formally unleashed on the world in my finest polyester. Was I in drag too?"

It was also in 1969 that—following two years of debate—the Government of Canada passed amendments to the Criminal Code—Bill C-150—that have since been heralded as the decriminalization of homosexuality. The bill, introduced by then-Justice Minister Pierre Trudeau, led to Trudeau's often-cited "There's no place for the state in the bedrooms of the nation" quote (which continues: "...and I think that what's done in private between adults doesn't concern the criminal code; when it's public it's a different matter.") The legislation passed, despite opposition from the Canadian Association of Chiefs of Police, who voted against any changes to laws regarding homosexuality.

But the bill did not, in fact, rescind the buggery or gross indecency laws, both used to criminalize gay sex. Instead it created an exception clause allowing two adults aged twenty-one and older to engage in gay sex in the privacy of their home. This meant inclusion—provided we assimilated and mirrored "normative heterosexual relations as closely as possible," Tim Hooper, Gary Kinsman, and Karen Pearlston wrote for the FAQ on anti-69.ca.

According to historian Tom Hooper, a member of the "Anti-69: Against the Mythologies of the 1969 Criminal Code Reforms" activist network, "criminal charges for consensual gay sex among adults increased in the decades after 1969, dramatically." Yet as I write this, in spring 2019, there has been much fanfare about the fiftieth anniversary of the supposed "decriminalization of homosexuality" in Canada. The government has even released a commemorative coin.

▼

Canada's first (known) gay group—the Association for Social Knowledge (ASK) in Vancouver—was founded in 1964. The following year, a man who would become central to the debate around Canada's laws around gay sex, Everett George Klippert, confessed to having consensual sex with another man on four separate occasions in the Northwest Territories; he had previously served three years after being convicted of gross indecency in Calgary. Klippert was sentenced as a dangerous sexual offender, allowing for his indefinite detention. In 1967 the Supreme Court of Canada upheld Klippert's dangerous sexual offender status. The Criminal Code reforms did not have an impact on Everett's case as they had no direct relation to the dangerous sexual offender provision. Klippert had also been arrested for having sex in public places (including in his car) and with people under the age of twenty-one (including when he was underage). He wouldn't be paroled until 1971.

Halifax's GAE wasn't the only organization to answer the clarion call of gay and trans liberation in the early 1970s. The country's first known trans group—the Association of Canadian Transexuals (ACT)—was formed in 1970 and in 1971 *The Body Politic*, the country's gay newspaper of record, would publish its first issue.

That same year, Toronto Gay Action (TGA) coordinated the seminal "We Demand" demonstration on Parliament. In the introduction to the 2017 anthology *We Still Demand: Redefining Resistance in Sex and Gender Struggles*—edited by Patrizia Gentile, Gary Kinsman, and L. Pauline Rankin—the rally "sought to oppose the [limitations of the] Criminal Code reforms by protesting against the higher age of consent for same-gender erotic practices, police repression, the national security campaigns against queers under way in the public service and the military, and [to call] for the repeal of gross indecency laws."

This burgeoning North American movement for gay liberation built upon the zeal of the 1960s movements for civil rights, against the Vietnam War, for both Black and Red Power (the latter a First Nations movement for self-determination), and women's rights.

In his autobiography, African-Nova Scotian civil rights activist and lawyer Burnley "Rocky" Jones (and his co-author James W. St.G. Walker) wrote: "Tariq Ali wrote a book about 1968, the great year of revolution around the world. It doesn't even mention Canada. Well, we had our own 1968 in Canada." For Rocky, the most "exciting part of that revolutionary year" began with the Congress of Black Writers, held in Montreal. The Congress was a historic gathering of Black radicals that included Black Panther Stokely Carmichael, South African singer and civil rights activist Miriam Makeba, Black writer and socialist activist C. L. R. James, and Rocky. The very next year Montreal would be the site of the Sir George Williams student protest: a thirteen-day occupation of the Computer Science building (at what is now Concordia University)—a result of the university's failure to take action against a racist professor whom several West Indian students had accused of unfair grading.

In 1969 the Trudeau government released the now-notorious White Paper, which, according to the Anti-69 organizing committee, "advocated for the elimination of all treaty rights protected by the Indian Act, and the assimilation of all Indigenous people into a homogeneous and white dominated Canadian society." Opposition from Indigenous communities across the country forced the government to withdraw the policy, and at home in Nova Scotia, led to the creation of several Mi'kmaw rights groups.

According to *Groups Dynamic: A Collection of Nova Scotia Her-Stories* published by the Canadian Congress for Learning Opportunities for Women (CCLOW) in 1990, the Nova Scotia branch of Voice of Women—a "cross-Canada network linking women to build a world founded on peace and justice"—took root in noted peace activist and two-time-NDP candidate Muriel Duckworth's living room in November 1960.

In 1965 Rocky Jones, along with Joan Jones (who died in 2019) and Dave Tarlow, founded The Nova Scotia Project—this province's answer to the African-American civil rights movement. The group is perhaps best known for its youth wing, Kwacha House, featured in the NFB film *Encounter at Kwacha House*, in which a young Walter Borden—a gay, Africadian/Mi'kmaw activist and actor—has the last word. The Project's founding coincided with the forced relocation of residents of the African-Nova Scotian community of Africville and the destruction of its homes and church, which took place in Halifax between 1964 and 1967.

In 1965 Walter was at Halifax's Cornwallis Street Baptist Church when Rocky pitched the Project to the congregation. Not long thereafter, Walter, a teacher at the time, attended his first meeting.

"There was no wavering in terms of my thinking," he says of the Project. "It was immediate; it was permanent."

"Within the Project there were those of us who were gay," he says. "It was never an issue. Ever." He never had to come out because he was never "in."

"I was who I was," he says.

The Nova Scotia Project tackled racism—in employment, in housing, and more—head on. The group would, for instance, send three couples—one Black, one white, and one mixed—to view a rental unit, compare how they were treated, and challenge the landlord if there was an inkling of discrimination.

The strategies employed by the civil rights movement "were used thereafter by every other group, whether it be feminists, whether it be gay," says Walter. "Which was fine, because if it works over here it's going to work over here."

Walter describes the period from the 1960s to the mid-1970s as a time when "the fire was there, everywhere." He spent the late 1960s studying acting in New York, were he was swept up in the anti–Vietnam War marches.

And then things changed.

"There was backlash to the whole Nixonian era and people were tired mentally," he says. "They were tired from the momentum of the '60s and early '70s and pulled away from it."

▼

For gay men during the 1960s and early 1970s, cruising—walking or driving around a public area looking for sex—was an important way to connect with other gays.

"Community was basically a cruising scene," GAE founding member Jim DeYoung said in an interview with Bill Pusztai for the GayHalifax wiki. Jim started cruising on and around Citadel Hill and the Halifax Commons—amongst the bleachers on the baseball field and near the brick building most recently known as The Pavilion—in the mid-to-late 1960s. Many of the people he picked up were sailors. Sometimes, if he didn't pick up, it was a case of—"Doesn't look like there's much around tonight; want to go for a coffee?"

Other Hali-famous cruising areas included The Triangle (the streets bordered by Queen Street, Dresden Row, and Spring Garden Road, which Robin Metcalfe dubbed the "cruising capital of the East" in a *Body Politic* article), Camp Hill Cemetery, the Public Gardens (or "Pubic Gardens" as it was colloquially known), and the Meat Rack (a low brick wall at the intersection of South Park Street and Spring Garden Road). Often, African-Nova Scotian gay man and former GAE executive member Chris Shepherd told me in an interview, the Meat Rack was more about socializing than picking up.

In a 1978 article about an upcoming national conference for lesbians and gay men in Halifax, *The Body Politic* wrote: "This city offers a unique opportunity to join a two-hundred-year-old cruising tradition on Citadel Hill in the heart of the downtown. If the action fails, there's always the view."

The article suggested come-from-aways looking for something "a little more off the beaten path (so to speak)" could visit Black Rock Beach at Point Pleasant Park—at their own risk, as "straights" also frequented the area. For those looking for a "tearoom trade" (slang for bathroom sex) the article suggested the Halifax Shopping Centre.

Jim noted that when an area became well known and gay-bashers moved in, they would relocate.

"Besides giving heterosexual thugs ('queer-bashers') a chance to beat or kill gays, this practice also leaves gays open to arrest," Robin Metcalfe wrote in an article on gays and the law in the 1976 "gay supplement" to Dalhousie University's student-run newspaper, the *Dalhousie Gazette*.

It wasn't only homophobic members of the public who gave these gay men a hard time, wrote Robin. "Rude cops will drive up, bark out 'c'mere,' demand identification, tell us to move on, ask why we are where we are, etc."

"You can't divide community and sex," Robin said later in an interview, stressing the importance of sexual networks for developing community space and identity.

▼

Carol Millet didn't know any other gays or lesbians before she went to Mount Saint Vincent University (MSVU)—that rumoured hotbed of lesbian activity—in the early 1970s. When she moved on-campus in her second year, there were at least four lesbians in her townhouse, which was home to somewhere between twelve and twenty women. They were the first people Carol came out to, and it was at the Mount that she had her first lesbian relationship. There weren't any formal groupings of gays and lesbians at the Mount then, says Carol, who graduated in 1974, and she and her peers socialized via plain old house parties.

"Then there were a lot of house parties, because a lot of women wouldn't go to clubs," says Nancy Brister.

"The men would go to the gay bars because they could afford to more than the women," Carol adds.

Katherine MacNeil—who moved from Cape Breton also to attend the Mount—found out about these lesbian dinner parties from an unusual source: her boyfriend. Katherine had enrolled at the Mount in the hope of finding other lesbians, but it hadn't happened.

"I was dating this guy, off and on, and he knew I was really gay—that I really shouldn't be going out with him," says Katherine. Her boyfriend put her in touch with a lesbian in her fifties who set her up with a friend who had come to Halifax from California. Their first (blind) date was at a dinner party.

"Oh, I was walking three feet off the ground," she says with a laugh. "I was very, very, very happy. Just the idea of having a date with another woman was super exciting."

Those regular soirees provided plenty of fodder for flirting, says Katherine, and nearly every dinner guest had already dated someone else in the room.

▼

In Anne's Fulton's archives there is a handwritten note that includes a list of the city's first gay bars: Club 777, Thee Klub, Granville Lunch, and PJ's Fast Food.

Nancy Brister stumbled upon Club 777, the first gay club located in the Green Lantern building (1585 Barrington Street) by way of the GAE's new phone line, Gayline, launched in October 1973 to provide information and referrals to the province's LGB population.

"I was in Halifax trying desperately to meet some women, and I couldn't," Nancy says.

Originally from the Annapolis Valley, Nancy had lived above a gay club on Church Street in Toronto while studying photographic arts at Ryerson Institute of Technology in the late 1950s and early 1960s. She used to watch lesbian couples go in and out of the club. "At first you couldn't really tell that they were both women. They were really into butch and femme."

The person on the other end of the Gayline told her that one of the men who lived in the Green Lantern would meet her and bring her to the women who frequented the club. The man, Nancy says, was GAE founding member and future owner of the city's first LGB bookstore, Tom Burns.

Nancy paced back and forth in front of the door on Barrington for what "felt like a hundred times" until finally, she thought, "Nobody's watching. Quick, duck in." She was terrified.

Tom led Nancy to a table of eight or so women against the back wall: *the table of women.* They were having a great time.

"It was just wonderful to meet them and find my community," says Nancy.

In those days, she says, when you met other gay and lesbian folks, you didn't give your real name, because you could lose your job or even your children if others learned of your sexual orientation. But the handful of women Nancy found via Club 777 became close, and eventually did reveal their true identities. Not long after they met, Nancy and a handful of other women—who met at the club, or at parties—formed a consciousness-raising group.

As more women—many of them university students—started coming out, the lesbian landscape of the city changed. "We sort of divided into our own groups," Nancy says. Up until then, "we were being held together by necessity. We were it."

The back room at the Stockade Restaurant on Windsor Street, near the Halifax Forum, was another gay bar. In order to get to it, patrons had to walk through the restaurant—something Carol describes as "depressing." "People felt that it added to the whole stigma of being gay or lesbian because you had to walk though the restaurant, and of course people would stare at you," she says. She only went once or twice, because "it just seemed so weird." But all of the bars were depressing, she says, except for The Turret and Rumours.

Anne's list also included "the straight businesses" that LGB folks frequented: the Candlelight Lounge on Spring Garden Road, Piccadilly Tavern and Grill on Grafton Street, and the LBR (the Lord Nelson's "Ladies' Beverage Room"—now the Oasis Pub—on Spring Garden Road).

In 2007 Greg Nepean published a paper featuring an anonymous Mi'kmaw two-spirit man, whom Greg calls "X." X told Greg about the sexual encounters that took place in the downstairs bathrooms of the Candlelight Lounge, which were frequented primarily by closeted married men in their thirties and forties. The Piccadilly Tavern and Grill—"the Old Pic" Lorne Izzard calls it—was a dumpy but "great" old tavern frequented by queers, bikers, and sex workers; it even allowed pets—dogs, rabbits, and even snakes. Anybody could go to the Old Pic, says Lorne. "They were way ahead of their time." Jim DeYoung first went to the Piccadilly at age sixteen. In the 1980s the owners converted the beloved dive into a modern disco. While the disco didn't attract the bikers, or menagerie of animals, the "New Pic" couldn't "care less if you were gay, straight, or in-between," says Lorne. Walter also remembers the New Service restaurant, a clandestine gathering spot on Argyle Street, where the Neptune Theatre is now.

In 1961 Nova Scotia's liquor law was amended to allow women into "ladies' beverage rooms" with a male escort, and in 1963 the Lord Nelson

Hotel opened its Ladies' Beverage Room. Though I did not interview anyone for this book who had actually been to the LBR, Deborah Trask remembers working-class women showing up at The Turret after they had been to the Beverage Room.

There was another bar, Nancy tells me, where the lesbians outnumbered the gay men: the beverage room on the first floor of the Dresden Arms Hotel. They were "quite out," she says of the women who frequented the establishment, and took up a "good portion" of the tables. People from the hotel used to come down to watch the lesbians, Nancy remembers. The women started going to the Dresden Arms because they were no longer welcome at their previous spot.

Throughout the 1970s, LGB Haligonians also patronized bars and restaurants such as The Seahorse Tavern on Argyle Street, The Garden View restaurant on Spring Garden Road, the Lobster Trap Cabaret on Brunswick Street, The Jury Room on Argyle Street, and a German restaurant called The Heidelberg on Dresden Row.

Nancy Brister in the 1980s. **(NANCY BRISTER COLLECTION)**

"As I say, these places cropped up when there was a need," Nancy says. "If we were asked to move along by one place, we needed another place."

▼

The first stop for many LGB folks when they first came out in the early to mid-1970s was one of two bars run by David Gray in the Green Lantern building at 1585 Barrington Street. Club 777 was originally situated farther North on Barrington, across from Camille's Fish and Chips. David bought and moved it to the Green Lantern building, says Tom Burns. In a 1983 taped conversation between Robin Metcalfe, Anne Fulton, and Diane Warren, they say Club 777, originally run by a group of gays, opened on New Year's Eve in 1970. The second iteration of the club was simply referred to as "Thee Klub" or by its nickname, "David's."

The Green Lantern building became "the hub of the gay community" in 1971 and '72, says Tom.

Tom was one of a handful of gay men who lived in the not-entirely-legal offices-turned-apartments in the building. David and his mother lived just upstairs, and three soon-to-be founding members of GAE—Tommy Miller, Nils Clausson, and Jim DeYoung—also called the building home. The man who owned the building was pretty liberal, and David had say over who lived there, says Tom.

Tom Burns at Thee Klub, Halloween 1972. (TOM BURNS COLLECTION)

Once, city officials dropped by to inspect the "offices," so the residents scrambled to hide their personal effects and to move the desks and chairs back in to camouflage their living quarters.

Thee Klub wasn't licensed and was only open two to three nights a week. There was a lounge area with wicker furniture and a small dance floor. It was the nicest club around in those days, says Tom.

There was a movie theatre nearby, and in order to avoid being seen, Thee

Klub hopefuls would have to wait until those crowds had dispersed. It was a "late-night sneakabout," says former GAE Executive member Chris Shepherd, who first went to David's in 1974. It was the "only game in town, and I suppose in 1974 you considered yourself lucky to have a game in town," he says.

"I did what many people did," says Chris. "Walked up and down the street until you saw a break in the traffic and no one on the sidewalk, and then you dashed in."

It was "liberating" to be with other gay men and lesbians, says former David's regular Mike Sangster. "There wasn't the pressure to be straight; [to] pretend. You could let your hair down."

Because it was the 1970s you were also free to wear the type of jeans that were "poured onto your body. You could see a dimple on your legs," says Mike, of the men's attire.

Anne Fulton was living with a couple of drag queens for her first Halloween in the city. It was "quite a phenomenon," she wrote in notes that I found in her archives. "I was astounded by the excitement caused by the notion of dressing up like a feminine woman. Sewing machines were humming, straight pins were all over the place, there was primping and fussing and measuring, and wigs sat around."

Later that night, Anne and the queens made their way to the Green Lantern building for the main event: the club's annual Halloween Gala. Crowds that exceeded fire-regulation restrictions crammed themselves into what Anne described as "a disco closet hidden in the dark recesses of the Green Lantern building" and "watched these splendid butterflies who had emerged from their cocoons for the night." For some time, she noted, the most important annual event of the year in the gay and lesbian community was the crowing of Miss Drag Queen Halifax.

"Drag was so predominant that one of the first attempts within the lesbian community for recognition and equality was to stage a Drag King show to parallel the Drag Queen shows," Anne wrote in her archives. "The woman who looked like Bobby Darin, unfortunately, did not win."

For some time, Anne wrote, she was the only lesbian who frequented Club 777. Diane Warren and her partner—her first lover and the love of her life, Ann McMullin—were "one of the first lesbian couples" to go, according to her entry on the GayHalifax wiki. Diane and Ann fell in love in 1966, and had a daughter together in 1967. (They were together until Ann passed in 2008.) In 1971 Diane learned of Halifax's gay community while volunteering at the Halifax-based counselling, information, and referral Help Line, which had been launched in 1969.

"I didn't think there was anyone besides me and Ann around; didn't know anyone who was gay," she told Robin and Anne in 1983.

Diane and Ann would go on to be two of the founding members of GAE.

▼

Lorne Izzard came to Halifax for the Easter long weekend in 1974 and ended up staying for good. That weekend he managed to secure both a job and an apartment; he went to live with three friends on Cunard Street. Peace, love, happiness, and all that, he says.

Lorne knew there was a gay club in town, but it would be a year before he would get "the nerve" to go. Driving by Thee Klub with friends, he would be "salivating" to go, Lorne remembers. He could hear the music from the street; could see the men going in and out of the building.

It was during one of those drives with friends that one of his fellow passengers asked the driver to drop him off at the Thee Klub. "I guess tonight's the night," Lorne thought. At least he wouldn't have to go it alone.

Lorne remembers every step he took up to the third-floor club, the bass pulsing throughout the building, the happy-looking people when they were finally inside. There were about fifty there that night *and* it happened to be a night that they were serving liquor.

But it was, of course, all about the dancing.

"That was a thrill. The first time you get asked to dance, right?" says Lorne. "And it's not a girl from high school. It's actually a guy asking you to dance."

In the age of disco, there was no longer a need to leave room for the Holy Spirit. Mike says it was: "Wow! You're touching each other! You're holding each other!"

The first song Mike remembers hearing at Thee Klub wasn't a disco banger, but the sweet strains of "Midnight Train to Georgia" by Gladys Knight & the Pips—his favourite song for waltzing.

It would be midnight before the place would really fill up, says Lorne, when people who weren't "out" joined the fete.

"We used to joke that you could always tell gay people in Halifax because they were the ones with the bags under their eyes," Nancy says with a laugh.

Lorne met the people he calls his "extended family" at David's—people he's still friends with to this day.

His apartment became a safe place, particularly for the Black drag queens who would get ready at Lorne's before a night on the town. The tight-knit group "hung out together, partied together, ate together, travelled together." And those queens were *good*, remembers Lorne.

"The Black queens were very private," he says. They "kept mostly within the Black community, because they felt safer there."

"The original drag queens of Halifax would get really pissed off when the Black queens would come down, because they'd win the prizes," he says.

In 1976 David sold the club to Condon MacLeod, and the bar was re-named "Condon's."

According to Scott MacNeil's insightful essay about of the gay nightlife in the 1970s and '80s, "Reflections in a Mirror Ball" on the GayHalifax wiki, Condon gave the place a makeover, painting the interior high-gloss white and bringing in matching white wicker furniture, black lights, and white padded lightboxes where people could rest their drinks around the dance floor.

"The large mirror ball spinning in front of the mirrored wall made the entire room sparkle," Scott wrote.

The club operated with an "occasional party" liquor licence, with the purpose of raising funds for the Equality Scholarship Fund, which went to a gay student entering university. That particular license was only granted every second week, and Condon would use a different business name on each application and send it to a different person each time he applied, writes Scott.

After Condon MacLeod—who went on to create well-known all ages spaces such as Café Ole and the Pavilion—bought the club, Lorne ascended the ranks to DJ. It was fun, Lorne says, but he hated not being able to get down on the dance floor. Sometimes, though, he would put on an eight-minute disco mix just so he could have a drink and dance.

In "Reflections in a Mirror Ball," Scott wrote: "One evening, a group of well-groomed, tanned, and trendy men arrived unannounced. Who were they?

All new faces. Air Canada had opened a flight attendant base in Halifax, and the boys were in town." Those beautiful, worldly "boys" became the talk of the gay community.

Once in awhile, Scott writes, Condon would host movie screenings on Sunday nights, projecting films on a white bedsheet suspended from the ceiling. The films included *Fortune and Men's Eyes*, a 1971 movie about a young man's experiences in prison, which features several gay characters, and *The Ritz*, released in 1976 and centred around a gay bathhouse.

The club's demise came after one of Condon's messengers to the Nova Scotia Liquor Licence Board let it slip that the licence was for a gay club. A few weeks later, a fire inspector visited and posted a notice that the venue had a maximum capacity of seventy-five people. On a weekend when they were serving liquor, more than two hundred people might be crammed into the space. The bar couldn't stay afloat.

"Sadly, the elevator no longer carried partygoers up to the top floor," Scott wrote.

Chapter 2

THE ACTIVISTS EMERGE: BIRTH OF THE GAE

(1972–1975)

"This letter is to inform you that Halifax has now stepped into the ever-expanding movement for gay liberation," began a typewritten letter signed by Anne Fulton, who was at that time the secretary of a newly minted organization called the Gay Alliance for Equality (GAE).

The "newsletter" was one of the gems I found in the box containing Anne's personal archives housed at Robin Metcalfe's Halifax apartment. In that box are some of the earliest artifacts of a movement for gay and lesbian liberation in the city—documents and materials not found in the provincial archives.

Tucked inside a vintage Sobeys bag (one with the green and orange logo) was a deceivingly inconspicuous black Duo-Tang. Inside, the words "GAY LIBERATION"—typed in bright red—jump out from an otherwise blank cover page. This Duo-Tang contains the minutes from the yet-to-be-named GAE— which first met in the Green Lantern building in May 1972—simply titled "Minutes of the Weekly Meeting: Gay Liberation." In June 1972 the membership elected the group's first steering committee: Tom Burns as chairman; Anne became secretary; Bernie Feener, vice-chair; Al La Forte, treasurer;

November 1972.

N E W S L E T T E R.

This letter is to inform you that Halifax has now stepped into the ever-expanding movement for Gay Liberation.

As of June 4th., 1972, the Halifax Gay community established an organization known as the Gay Alliance for Equality, with an elected executive committee of five. We plan to register as a non-profit organization in the near future, and we will be working with, and through the community to better facilitate gay - community relations.

We are yet a new and struggling organization and have few and modest accomplishments to stand with our name. Therefore, at this point, and in the future we would appreciate any correspondence and ideas which we could incorporate into our program.

Looking forward to hearing from you,

GAY ALLIANCE FOR EQUALITY

M. Anne Fulton
Secretary.

Suite 207,
1585 Barrington Street,
Halifax. Nova Scotia.
Canada.

A newsletter announcing the establishment of the GAE, dated November 1972.
(ANNE FULTON ARCHIVES)

and Cynthia Watts (who Jim DeYoung notes was from Australia and used a wheelchair), the community relations officer.

That same month, representatives from Halifax travelled to Ottawa for a national strategy session with gay groups from Vancouver, Ontario, Montreal, and Quebec City. According to the letter, dated November 1972, Halifax's first official gay advocacy group was established on June 4 of that year.

For the east coast gay group, "gay liberation," according to a statement released in 1973, referred to "both an affirmation of the right to live as we choose and an intent to extend that right to others."

The same year GAE coalesced, some members of Toronto's gay community organized that city's first Gay Pride week to observe the one-year anniversary of the "We Demand" march. The Association of Canadian Transexuals (ACT) along with the Community Homophile Association of Toronto (CHAT) held a forum on transexuality.

Anne detailed the origins of those first GAE meetings in a handwritten note in Robin's Sheet Harbour collection.

In spring 1972 Anne had stumbled upon a photocopied poster that read: "It's Time for Gay Liberation," advertising an upcoming gay liberation meeting in Halifax. "I thought WOW!" Anne told Diane and Robin in a 1983 conversation recorded and archived by Robin. The meeting was organized by Frank Abbott—a Dartmouth-raised member of CHAT, who had moved to Toronto after graduating from Saint Mary's University in Halifax—during a trip home to visit family.

Anne had been searching for "community"—first in the butch/femme bar scene in Saint John, New Brunswick, and later at Club 777 in Halifax—so she attended the meeting. About fourteen people (all men, aside from Anne) attended, including club owner and future GAE chairman David Gray, future GAE chairman and owner of the city's first gay bookstore, Tom Burns, Dalhousie PhD student Nils Clausson, and an international student from China.

After the meeting, Anne and Frank strolled home down Rainnie Drive; Frank put his arm around her before they parted ways.

"I had the very distinct feeling of having been passed the torch of gay liberation," Anne wrote in 1981. "And I believe I've carried the torch for many years since then. (Burnt myself with it a few times too.)"

▼

Tom Burns was the first GAE founding member I met in person. We met in his apartment in Halifax, where we were surrounded by his extensive collection of records—a collection he started in 1964.

Tom, who grew up in Halifax, got involved in the GAE to "help gay people understand that they're not alone," he says. "I thought I was the only person in the world like this." Even in Halifax, people outright denied that there were, in fact, gays living within city limits. "They live[d] in Montreal and Toronto, maybe," says Tom. He dropped out of vocational school because of the homophobia—the whispers. "Oh, he's queer; he's queer," he mimics in a hushed tone. For him, GAE was all about educating people, primarily non-gays. "In those days, if you were queer, homosexual implied "sexual." So all you wanted to do [was] run around wanting to have sex with everybody. That kind of nonsense."

When GAE officially incorporated in 1973, its first three objectives were: "to promote education [on] all aspects of homosexuality"; "to educate the public regarding problems confronting the homosexual"; and "to work for changes in the prevailing attitudes of society towards homosexuality." GAE also continued to be a player on a national level, as one of the sixteen groups that constituted the National Gay Election Coalition (NGEC), a group coordinated by Toronto Gay Action to bring gay issues into the campaign leading up to the October 1972 federal election. (GAE reps attended another national meeting of "homophile" and "gay liberation" groups to discuss political action and organization in May 1973.)

For Anne, the founding of GAE marked the injection of some politics into Halifax's gay community. And with that, she wrote, "a new breed of people began to emerge.... Those who were good with words, speaking, writing and organizing became important."

It was at the GAE and at the lesbian drop-in at the Brenton Street Women's Centre—the one started by Nancy Brister—that Anne finally met more women like herself and began to find her community.

"Gay liberation was invigorating," she wrote. "I felt proud, energized, and validated. I was a woman with a mission."

Those first recorded conversations of the soon-to-be named GAE were dominated by the logistics of setting up a new group and recruiting members. Attendance at meetings ranged from eight people, to seventeen, to as many as thirty. By February 1973, half of the people on the six-person executive were women; the director of the phone line was also a woman.

In a 1973 interview with the *Dalhousie Gazette*, Nils Clausson told the paper that "assistance of gays is largely a matter of liberation through pride." He added that attending GAE meetings could help "increase the confidence of members through participation in activities with serious social and political aims."

Establishing a political agenda for the group had its challenges. During a discussion about the "gay spirit" at one of the group's earliest meetings, it was concluded "that gays in Halifax should get involved in things which concern their social environment and that at the present time very few have any interest in anything else but cruising."

During the same meeting, members spoke of increased surveillance of local cruising areas, heightened harassment by both the public and police, and the group's efforts to contact a lawyer to brief them on their legal rights.

It wasn't long after Diane and Ann's first foray to the club that they realized "that things were tough for gays in the Halifax area."

"Many of our friends and acquaintances landed up at the V. G. emergency!!" Diane wrote on the GayHalifax wiki, referring to the emergency department at Halifax's Victoria General Hospital. She added that "there was no police support."

When she was twenty years old Mary Ann Mancini moved to Halifax from Sackville, New Brunswick. "We were in a time period where the cops were allowed to beat you up, you were allowed to be kicked out of your apartment, you were allowed to be kicked out of your jobs. And nobody said anything," she told journalist Allie Jaynes in an interview for the GayHalifax wiki that was never published. (After Mary Ann died, Allie allowed me to use parts of her interview for this book.)

"Nobody cared; it was like—it's only the queers," Mary Ann said. "Of course you're allowed to go queer-bash, it was just an everyday sport."

Gay bashing was part of the impetus for founding GAE, said Jim DeYoung. "The only way you could do something about it was if you had numbers," he said in his interview with Bill Pusztai for the GayHalifax wiki. "The only way you had numbers [was] if you had an organization that people could belong to."

One of the first things the fledgling group did was to set up a phone line that was known as the Gayline, says Tom. A 1983 report written by Anne Fulton, who was at that time the director of the Gayline, gave credit to Diane Warren for the idea to establish this service. Diane had spent several years answering the phones for Halifax's Help Line, and says she "became aware of the need for a phone line of our own, with our own specific resources and our own understanding of and hopes for our situation within society."

Before they had even decided upon a name, Anne had checked with the city's Help Line and learned that they did indeed receive calls from gays. According to her own notes, when Anne had called the Help Line earlier that year looking for the gay and lesbian community in Halifax, she had been given the address of the Mattachine Society, all the way in New York City. Founded in 1950, the society was one of the first (known) gay rights groups in the United States. Later, when the GAE was drafting its constitution, the Mattachine Society would send a copy of its own to act as a template.

When Halifax's Help Line requested a phone number to which they could refer gay callers, the GAE offered up a group member's home phone number. The GAE officially launched the Gayline—housed in a four-by-six-foot room in the Green Lantern building—in October 1973. The line was primarily funded by Club 777 and Thee Klub owner David Gray, who took up a collection at the club, said Diane. GAE was responsible for raising the rest.

Staffed by somewhere between fifteen and twenty volunteers, the line ran from seven o'clock to ten o'clock on Thursday, Friday, and Saturday nights. Though they only got two or three calls a night—and sometimes no calls at all—at least it was there, says Tom.

In 1983 Diane told Anne and Robin that some of the male Gayline volunteers had tried to use the phone line "as a dating service," which led her to throw several of them off the line. In a Gayline training manual that I found in Anne Fulton's archives, the first point under "Rules for Counsellors" was: "The line is not a dating service."

The Gayline had been many people's entry point into the gay and lesbian community in Halifax; it would later be at the centre of one of the GAE's most public battles.

▼

In the 1972 letter announcing the GAE's arrival, Anne characterized the group as a "new and struggling organization" with "few and modest accomplishments to stand with our name."

In October 1973 the Registry of Joint Stock Companies denied GAE's request to incorporate, as the Registry "did not understand our intentions and how we would fulfill our ideas," according to GAE minutes. The group was, however, incorporated just a month later on November 19. In those early years, GAE met twice a month, either at the Green Lantern building or at Diane and Ann's home; later, after David stepped down as chairman, members stopped meeting at the club and moved to the Universalist Unitarian Church.

The fact that GAE spelled out "gay" was intentional, says Tom, who had pitched the name. The first official name was the "Alliance for Gay Equality," or AGE, which had beat out "Alliance for Gay Dignity" by one vote.

"We felt at the time that this would encompass all gays, male and female," Diane, who was chairman at the time of incorporation, wrote. "It should be noted that there was still hostility between male and female gays!!"

The founding officers were an almost-even split of men and women, and included one Mi'kmaw woman, whose name did not resurface in any other documents or interviews. Many of the founding officers lived together in a handful of houses in both north and south end Halifax.

"When denied the use of The Club [sic] for our meetings, we met at my home, many hours were spent there drafting petitions and letters for things we wanted changed or done to enable us to be recognized as normal, self-respecting human beings and not as the deviant, aberrant creatures society felt and or wanted us to be!!" Diane wrote of those early years.

Although it's not clear how it came about, GAE members began speaking to psychology and nursing students at Dalhousie and Saint Mary's universities. It was a "breakthrough" for the group, says Tom.

"That generation started to listen," he says. "Instead of talking 'about,' they started talking 'to'." Unfortunately that wasn't always the case; in 1973 the GAE intervened when the Saint Mary's University student council adopted a policy barring same-sex couples from attending its events.

During Tom's term as chairman, the local CBC Television news program did a piece on the new group, showing members working the phone line and dancing at Thee Klub. At first Tom was hesitant to appear on-air, as he wasn't out to his entire family. He remembers thinking, "If I'm chairperson of the GAE, I've got to come out." So he did—and "that was it."

According to Tom, that first cohort of GAE activists focused their energies on two main issues, one of which was sexual orientation in the provincial Human Rights Act.

On March 5, 1973, a full twenty-three years before sexual orientation was finally included in the Nova Scotia Human Rights Act, members of GAE presented a paper they called "A Brief Regarding the Human Rights Act" to the Nova Scotia Legislature.

Drafted by the GAE's Legal Reform Committee (consisting of Nils, David, and Clyde Richardson, a GAE member who would later become chair), the brief commended the government for prohibiting discrimination based on race, religion, creed, colour, sex, or ethnic or national origin. It went on to argue, however, that in order to be "fully consistent with the noble principle that all members of the human family partake of an inherent dignity and human rights, the Nova Scotia Human Rights Act must be amended to include sexual orientation as grounds on which discrimination is prohibited."

In a press release, the Alliance—not yet a year old—said that members hoped changing the Act would be a step "towards ending the oppression of homosexuals by a society which knows virtually nothing of this minority." The release went on to quote influential African-American queer writer James Baldwin, stating, "If you fall in love with a boy, you fall in love with a boy. The fact that Americans consider it a disease says more about them than it says about homosexuality."

On March 28, five GAE representatives met with members of the Nova Scotia Human Rights Commission to discuss their proposal, at which point the Commission told them that no action would be taken.

First, commission staff told GAE activists that sexual orientation could not be included in the Act for two seemingly contradictory reasons: because there were not enough documented cases of discrimination against LGB folks, and because the commission did not have the staff to handle an increase in complaints.

"The Human Rights people said, 'No, no, we have too much to do here; you guys aren't discriminated against anyways,'" Tom recalls.

Lastly, the commission told GAE reps that the rights of Black and Indigenous peoples "must take precedence over those of other minorities," effectively pitting marginalized groups against one another and ignoring the fact that an individual could be both or all of the above. In response, Nils wrote in a letter to MLA Bill Gillis that the GAE unconditionally supported the efforts of Black and Indigenous peoples, adding: "To achieve justice and equality, we do not believe that the Nova Scotia Government should pursue a policy in which the rights of some minorities are protected at the price of having the rights of other minorities totally unprotected."

For the gay liberationists the issue was clear; they wrote: "Either the Nova Scotia Government condones discrimination against gays or it does not."

Despite the dearth of legal protection for LGB folks, in 1974 the GAE wrote to the training and personnel officer for the City of Halifax, saying that "it has come to the attention of the Gay Alliance for Equality that several employees of the city of Halifax, whose sexual orientation happens to be homosexual, fear that, should their sexual orientation become known to their superiors, they will be dismissed." The letter went on to ask the city to "state, as carefully and completely as possible, what the City's policy, stated or implicitly understood, is on this matter." The letter notes that at the time GAE did not know of anyone who had been denied a job or a promotion, or who had been fired because of their sexuality. The group sent a similar letter to the province's civil service commission asking if the government had any policy "either stated or implied" which permitted discrimination against prospective or current employees based on their sexual orientation, and asking them to issue a public statement acknowledging as much.

In March of that year the GAE took its fight to the provincial election by issuing a candidate questionnaire on gay rights. Off the bat, the group informed political hopefuls: "Should you choose not to return the questionnaire we will conclude that you do not consider the civil rights of homosexuals worthy of your attention, and that you condone existing discriminatory policies and practices affecting homosexuals, and believe that there is nothing wrong if a homosexual lives in the fear that if his or her sexual preference became known he could lose his job, or be denied a position or promotion commensurate with his abilities as a citizen of a free society."

The survey—entitled simply "Gay Political Action Campaign"—asked the candidates if they supported the Alliance's recommendation that the Human Rights Act should be amended to "protect homosexuals from discrimination in employment, housing and public accommodation." It asked if they thought the government should adopt a resolution prohibiting discrimination against LGB employees. It asked if they were in favour of a national policy that ensured that LGB people were treated equally in the areas of employment and housing, and whether they thought that homosexuality should be discussed in sex-ed classes in public schools in the province.

Twenty-two candidates responded to the survey: three Liberals, five Progressive Conservatives, and thirteen New Democrats. Two Liberals supported gay rights, while one wanted more information. Three Progressive Conservatives supported the GAE, while one found the questions to be "unfair." Twelve NDP candidates were on-board, while one exclaimed, "You'll get no support from me!" None of the three party leaders responded.

▼

Another top priority for the GAE in those early days was ending the brutal practice of "conversion therapy," which was meant to "cure" people of their homosexuality. May 24, 1973, saw the publication of the GAE's first newsletter—"*GAE/Y Information Service.*" In it, Tom wrote about conversion therapy and the use of ESB electric stimulation (a form of electrotherapy), which—according to his article—was "now being investigated as an important new way of altering the behaviour of homosexuals." The article went on to describe "aversion therapy," in which gay men were shown pictures of attractive naked men on a screen and then given an electric shock which stopped when the image was replaced with that of a naked woman.

"Where our existing sexual standards deny people the right to happiness, freedom, and love, we would do better to change our standards than try to change our fellow human beings," Tom concluded.

Diane remembers a meeting with representatives of Victoria General's psychiatry department just before the American Psychiatric Association delisted homosexuality as a mental disorder, an early victory of the gay liberation movement. (They replaced it with "sexual orientation disturbance disorder.")

"They were really amazed that we were so together," she said. "They went around and around and around, trying to find a chink. Like, there's got to be something wrong with y'as if you're gay."

"We saw people who went through conversion therapy," Tom says. "Saw what they used to be and what they were [after]."

> The issues of human rights protections and conversion therapy are not as far removed from our current reality as some would like to think. Although sexual orientation was finally included in the provincial Human Rights Act in 1991 (and in the federal Act in 1996), gender identity and expression were not included until 2012 in Nova Scotia, and until 2017 federally—meaning trans people did not formally have human rights in the eyes of the Government of Canada until just three years before this book was published.
>
> In the summer of 2018 the fight against conversion therapy was revisited when a Pictou County Bible camp attempted to bring in speakers from Coming Out Ministries, a group that advocates a "cure" for queerness. (The group did not come to Nova Scotia in the end, due to the immense public pressure.) Community outcry prompted the passing of provincial legislation in September 2018 which banned conversion therapy in the province (with some caveats).

▼

Running Nova Scotia's first gay group could be discouraging, says Tom; the Alliance sometimes struggled to get people to attend its meetings.

"There were guys that came to the club who would never come to a GAE meeting," Jim DeYoung said in his GayHalifax wiki interview. Some, including those who worked for the provincial or federal governments, wouldn't get involved because of their jobs.

The group's fundraising efforts—a bingo, a dance—didn't bring in any money, and "we couldn't seem to stop fighting with each other," Anne wrote in an undated note.

Some wanted to focus on the club scene and making money, says Tom, and that wasn't his goal, so he backed away.

"I didn't want to spend my time fighting other gay people," he says.

"Once again personalities began to cause problems," Diane wrote on the GayHalifax wiki. "We had our right-wingers; left-wingers; middle-of-the-road;

and our out & out vocal militants; our internal problems began to overtake the objectives that we had set out at incorporation!" There were many plays for power, Diane told Anne and Robin in 1983. "Everyone wanted to be the boss." Every night, Diane said, there would be "hours and hours of fighting and squabbling over the most asinine things. Who was going to have their name on the letterhead."

Diane resigned as chairman of GAE in 1974 when she decided to go back to university, and because, she said, of "the changes in ideology that were occurring."

She didn't have the heart to get involved again, she told Anne and Robin. "Nooooothing but a heartache," Anne crooned in response.

▼

Throughout our interview, Tom Burns sums up nearly every story—of founding Nova Scotia's first LGB advocacy group, of those early years, and of later opening the province's first LGB bookstore—with an impossibly humble "That's about it."

Most of all, Tom is proud of the role that he, the GAE, and The Alternate Book Shop played in helping other Nova Scotians come out.

"In those days there was all of this negativity around you, and all you would hear was 'queer' and 'cocksucker'," Tom reflects. "It was nice to have someone that you could talk to that knows what you're going through, [and] that would sit down and talk to you."

"I think I helped a few people along the way," he says.

Chapter 3

HOMOSEXUAL ACTIVITY

(1975–1979)

It was 1974, when he was living in Edmonton, Alberta, that Robin Metcalfe finally summoned the courage to look up "homosexuality" in a book in that city's public library. He remembers catching the bus home and thinking, "I'm allowed to look at men's bums!"

Emboldened, Robin attempted to contact the gay group in his home province of Nova Scotia, but GAE had ceased operations.

In 1975 Robin was working as a sleeping-car porter for CN Rail and during a stopover in Montreal he found old copies of the GAE newsletter at the office of an anglophone gay organization. One of the newsletters was a special issue about venereal diseases, and several of the articles had been penned by someone named "Val Dalrymple." Excited to finally have a contact name, Robin called all three Val Dalrymples listed in the phone book and "had some very curious conversations." What he didn't know was that the name Val Dalrymple was a stand-in for "VD," an abbreviation for venereal disease. Luckily, the newsletter also included an ad for a GAE meeting at the Universalist Unitarian Church in Halifax, whose minister put Robin in touch with one of GAE's founding members. That church, he notes, was the "first non-queer institution to give shelter and support to queer organizations" in the city.

In 1975, Tom Burns remember a mutual friend telling him, "This Robin guy wants to talk to you." They ended up talking on the phone for two and a half hours, met up a few days later and talked for another hour and a half. They've been friends since.

Robin's first gay stop in Nova Scotia was Thee Klub, which he went to with founding GAE member Robert Stout after Bob wrapped up an evening performance at Dalhousie University of *The Boys in the Band*, a groundbreaking play written in 1968 that portrayed a group of gay men celebrating a birthday in New York City.

The dance craze of the moment was "the bump," which entailed jumping, planting your feet, and bumping hips with your dance partner.

"I was staring at the floor a lot," remembers Robin. "I was too intimidated to make eye contact." Fortunately, he says, another David's patron wasn't too intimidated to make eye contact with him. He felt like a kid in a candy shop.

▼

Tom Burns views the early days of GAE as making way for the fervent activism that took place in the mid-to-late 1970s. It was a "torrent" of activity, says Robin.

The October 1975 GAE General Meeting was the first in nearly a year—"a year in which the Alliance had virtually died," according to the GAE's 1976 Annual Secretary's Report, which Robin authored. Since 1974, the GAE had been a member of the MOVEment for Citizens' Voice and Action—a coalition of community groups from areas that today are part of the Halifax Regional Municipality, aimed at providing resources (such as a meeting space, office supplies, and a coveted Gestetner duplicating machine) to its members. The GAE held meetings, open to all, in the MOVE offices on Argyle Street twice a month. MOVE, which had been co-founded by noted peace activist Muriel Duckworth, later housed the GAE's Gayline.

That year—1975—was also when Tom opened The Alternate Book Shop, "Atlantic Canada's gay book store," in the Green Lantern building. Located on the third floor, the store's hours on Thursday, Friday, Saturday, and Sunday nights corresponded with both Thee Klub's and the Gayline's.

In at interview with Robin for *The Body Politic*, Tom credits a visit to Glad Day Bookshop, currently the world's oldest LGBTQ bookstore, in Toronto, for the idea. Growing up, books had helped him come to terms

Two x - rated bibliographers; Jeannette Foster and Gene Damon, plus News, Reviews, Dykes, Flaunting it, and Classifieds.

75¢

THE

Body Politic

Gay Liberation Journal   No. 31 March

Gay murders unsolved
Can you help?

Six-city protest
against CBC ban

Fighting on beside him
A mother's work for gay rights

Robin Metcalfe, of Halifax
talks about coming out

The cover of the March 1977 issue of *The Body Politic*, with a feature story about Robin Metcalfe. **(ANNE FULTON ARCHIVES)** with his sexuality, and he thought that maybe a gay bookstore would help others do the same.

"Tom is less concerned with making a profit than with supplying a much-needed service by offering a source of information to the gay community, in line with his philosophy of 'liberation through education,'" Robin wrote in a November/December 1975 article in *The Body Politic* about the store, called "Liberation Through Education." "He hopes that the Bookshop will 'educate ourselves and others about us.'"

As noted in the *Body Politic* interview, the long, narrow store carried around a hundred titles, "ranging from women's and Gay Liberation books, periodicals, and newspapers, through gay fiction and special interest books, such as the biographies of popular entertainers, to soft porn and skin magazines." It carried books such as *The Frontrunner* by Patricia Nell Warren—the first gay novel to appear on the *New York Times* bestseller list. It also carried almost everything by well-known lesbian writer Gertrude Stein, plus materials such as the gay men's porn magazine *Mandate* and gay general interest magazine *The Advocate*, and, of course, *The Body Politic*.

"The first month I opened I lost two hundred dollars; the second month I opened I lost forty dollars. I kept losing," says Tom. But it was there, if people needed it. It was when he started selling "poppers," a liquid made from chemicals from the alkyl nitrite family, which gay men would sniff to loosen up for anal sex, that he started to make some money, and was able to pay himself twenty-five dollars a month. Years later, having moved across the street to the same building as The Turret, Tom sold the store to Emerald Gibson (who was also a drag performer known as Ezzie).

In 1975 the GAE built its membership back up to sixty-eight members, and in November the group re-launched the Gayline with the memorable number 429-6969.

"Because this is a gay line in a homophobic society, our existence is political," read a Gayline volunteer manual found in Anne Fulton's archives.

The line provided support as well as information on local gay or gay-friendly bars, restaurant, bathhouses, and other social activities; it also offered referrals to doctors, VD clinics, and legal resources.

The Gayline is how many LGB Haligonians—and many of the people I interviewed for this book—found out about the local gay scene and the GAE.

From November 1975 to October 1976 the Gayline received a total of 604 calls, 88 percent from men. The Gayline struggled to attract women volunteers.

Prank calls were an ongoing problem. In a 1983 Gayline report, Anne Fulton, who was the director of the phone line, wrote that pranks made up the majority of the calls received. She joked that her goal was to at least "attract a few original or inventive crank callers." In April of that year the line got a total of 889 calls—the highest monthly total in Gayline history. Anne attributed the spike partly to recent advertising in university newspapers, but also to the *Daily News*'s headline from the preceding week, which read: "Gay Plague Hits Metro."

"Sometimes I would just take it off the hook," says Anthony Trask, who staffed the GAE's office between 1979 and 1981, "which wasn't the greatest thing, but when you're getting those harassing calls, like ten in twenty minutes..." The digits "6969" had been picked as a joke, he says, but it contributed to the high number of harassing calls. The GAE office number was 429-4294, spelling out "GAY-GAY-4."

"The odd one was real," says Anthony, of the calls the line received. And there were the regular callers who "didn't know anyone else. They were either in a hetero relationship or too scared."

Nancy Brister volunteered on both the general Help Line and the Gayline. One night, at two or three o'clock in the morning, Nancy's home phone rang. When she picked it up, she heard something unexpected on the other end: her own voice counselling somebody. Suddenly the recording stopped and a male voice said, "I know where you live." Nancy hung up. She couldn't tell if it was a Help Line or a Gayline call, but both lines kept the locations of their offices and the identities of their volunteers secret.

"I quit both lines instantly," says Nancy. "It was—it was terrifying."

In May 1977 the Gayline received a bomb threat, and in 1982 Gayline director Emerald Gibson resigned after receiving death threats for an interview he had done with *Halifax Magazine*. His number was unlisted.

There are people who owe their lives to the Gayline, says Robin. He remembers a "husky working-class dyke" who used to crush him with a hug whenever she saw him, because he had been staffing the Gayline the night she'd called and said, "I might be a lesbian."

▼

"It seems like there was nothing and then there was everything," Mary Ann Mancini said of the mid-to-late 1970s.

In 1976 the GAE formed a Civil Rights Committee (CRC)—a political action wing of sorts.

The press release heralding the committee's formation read: "The committee will investigate and identify areas of anti-homosexual discrimination in legislation and politics on the provincial and municipal levels of government and by businesses and non-governmental agencies, and will work to end such discrimination. The committee will also seek to educate the Nova Scotia public and their elected representatives on the rights of the gay minority to such protection from discrimination as is now available to other minority groups."

That same year, GAE launched a short-lived monthly newsletter called *The Voice of Canada's Ocean Playground*. It was edited by Mary Ann Mancini, and an editorial on the front page of the first issue declared: "It's about time the one hundred thousand or more gay people in the Maritimes had a voice to call their own."

In *The Voice*'s second issue, Mary Anne wrote about the newly resurrected Speakers Bureau, in which "the members talk with any educational or social group interested in homosexuality," she explained. "Exposure to the Speakers Bureau of GAE may be the only chance many people have to confront a homosexual."

Mary Ann was driven to join the GAE's Speakers Bureau after a negative experience with a doctor.

When Mary Ann was twenty-six years old she had gone to a doctor to address her drinking problem. On her second visit, unbeknownst to her, the doctor had invited several of his colleagues in to ask her about being gay. Mary Ann—who had been taught to obey authority—talked for about an hour while they stared at her, she says. She didn't reach out for help for maybe two years after that. (Mary Ann, who became active within Gay AA, had been sober for over thirty years at the time of her death in 2019.)

That experience "made me think I was going to have a voice about being gay on my terms and I joined the Speakers Bureau and ended up doing a lot of classes at Dalhousie," Mary Ann told journalist Allie Jaynes in 2014.

"I think we were very successful with that group," Mary Ann said of the Speakers Bureau. "They would be so uptight when you walked into that class and they would be so into you by the time [you] left."

Mary Ann herself was technically a student in Dalhousie University's physical education program, but "majored in gay activism, because I didn't go there either," she says with a laugh. "Mostly gay activism is run by single people and college students and homeless people," Mary Ann told Jaynes. "It's the poor and the college students mostly, because they don't have anything to lose."

For Anthony Trask, who moved to the city from Wolfville when he was twenty-two, the Speakers Bureau allowed him to "reach people my age and explain whatever I could." He remembers one "slightly intimidating" Speakers Bureau talk he gave to a three-hundred-person class of Dalhousie University medical students. "Basically you're teaching these people how to treat homosexuality in their practice in this one-hour session," Anthony says.

In the days before one such university talk, a panicked young man approached Anthony at The Turret. Anthony was scheduled to talk to his class. "You don't know me. You've never seen me. Please—I'm begging you," the student pleaded, in tears.

"You were afraid for your life," says Anthony. Obligingly, Anthony completely ignored him during his presentation.

▼

In 1975 the GAE embarked on one of the most protracted political battles in the group's history—with a seemingly unlikely adversary: the Canadian Broadcasting Corporation (CBC).

In 1974 the GAE had tried to get a rather unremarkable PSA advertising the Gayline aired on CBC Halifax radio station CBH-FM. The PSA read: "The GAE Inc. is operating a counselling phone line for male and female homosexuals. The phone line is for problem-solving, giving out information and for referrals." It was not aired. The next year, the Alliance re-submitted the Public Service Announcement to the station.

Getting nothing but dead air from the broadcaster, GAE member and Gayline volunteer Robert Stout wrote the station asking them to "confirm that the following advert will be put on the radio or [provide] a refusal and reasoning."

Over the ensuing months—which eventually became years—the CBC offered a number of conflicting justifications for denying the PSA. In May 1976 the director of CBC Radio in the Maritimes, John McEwen, said he took issue with the word "counselling."

"There are a lot of people out there on the borderline between heterosexuality and homosexuality," McEwen was quoted saying in alternative newspaper *The 4th Estate*. "We have to be careful about what kind of counselling these people receive. The counselling these people get will have a great effect on their lives and family."

That following September McEwan told Allan Zdunich of the *Dalhousie Gazette* that the CBC didn't have room for the PSA, adding: "We can't promote just anything. We can't promote that sort of group."

According to an article in the May/June 1976 issue of *The Body Politic*, a representative of the Halifax station informed the GAE that the public broadcaster had a national policy "against accepting public announcements from homophile organizations," as they were "offensive to CBC's general audience." The corporation later disputed the GAE's claim that they had been told that, telling David Garmaise, the secretary of the National Gay Rights Coalition (NGRC), that there was no such policy. The official response was only issued after the NGRC made a series of phone calls and sent several letters to the CBC—including one to CBC president Al Johnson.

In that same letter, however, CBC Audience and Public Affairs vice-president Peter Meggs wrote: "The corporation additionally requires that any announcement must not promote or comment on any controversial issue." The decision to refuse the Gayline PSA, Meggs continued, was also due to the existence of the Help Line in Halifax, through which "homosexual callers are given full information about the Gay Alliance, its meetings and telephone number." The Help Line, Meggs argued, was available 24/7 whereas the Gayline was only available three nights a week.

Just one week into 1977, Meggs wrote the GAE to inform them that the crown corporation would continue to refuse their public service announcements due to the fact that "the request of your organization represents subject matter which is still considered controversial by our audiences."

That was it; the GAE was fed up and couldn't take it anymore. On February 17, 1977, the GAE set up a picket against the crown corporation on the sidewalks in front of the now-demolished CBC building at the corner of Sackville and South Park Streets. It was Nova Scotia's first known LGB picket.

The twenty-one-person protest was the first in a series that would be held clear across the country—in Montreal, Toronto, Ottawa, Winnipeg, and Vancouver—the first nationally coordinated gay and lesbian demonstration.

In Halifax, placards were scrawled with slogans such as "Gays Pay 10% of CBC's Budget: We Want Our Money's Worth", "Controversy = Bigotry" (this one was brandished by Jim MacSwain), and "End CBC Discrimination" (carried by Mary Ann Mancini).

"The airwaves are public property and the CBC is a publicly owned system," Robin said in a GAE press release. "It is supported by the taxes of Canadian citizens, many of whom are gay. It has a responsibility to give community groups fair and equal access to public service announcements without discrimination based upon prejudice. CBC has not fulfilled this responsibility and must be reminded of it."

During the campaign, the GAE received significant support from the *Dalhousie Gazette*, which initiated a student press boycott of CBC advertising; the boycott was officially adopted by the Canadian University Press (CUP) in 1977. This was significant, given that the seventy CUP-subscribed student newspapers across the country received ad revenue from the CBC.

"I don't support discrimination; I don't care how much it costs," said then-Dalhousie Student Union (DSU) President Gord Neal, himself a Black man.

In a letter to the editor, one *Gazette* reader wrote: "Are you turning this paper into the Dal Gay-zette? Almost since the beginning of this school year you have pressed upon us the terrible injustice being brought down upon the fags of Halifax. Who cares? No one I know." The letter closed, "Stop supporting a silly bowl of fruits, and start doing some real reporting."

In its response, the *Gazette* took the reader to task for their "immaturity and narrow-mindedness," adding: "Our support of the rights of the Gay Alliance for Equality In Halifax is much appreciated by them, and has spurred others across the country to fight for their deserved equal rights."

The CBC was not the only media outlet to deny GAE advertisements during the mid-to-late 1970s; two commercial radio stations, CHNS and CFDR, and the *Chronicle Herald/Mail Star* all rebuffed ads for the Gayline and

February 17, 1977: picketers protest the CBC's refusal to air the GAE's Gayline public service announcement. **(ROBIN METCALFE)**

GAE meetings. CHNS told *The 4th Estate* that it was a "family station" and, as such, couldn't promote the likes of the GAE or what it called "skin flicks." CFDR told the GAE that the PSA would offend its audience, and inquired as to whether the GAE "retained medical personnel who could help homosexuals to 'cure' themselves." *The 4th Estate*, the *Dartmouth Free Press*, and radio station CJCH were the only outlets that didn't reject the ad. But although the person responsible for PSAs at CJCH said they saw "no reason this group shouldn't be treated like any other group" and that they "shouldn't be discriminated against," members of the GAE noted that at least one of the CJCH announcers read the PSA in a "distorted and farcical" way.

The local CBC station's pending CRTC licence renewal, and the accompanying public hearings, made the CBC a more strategic target for a campaign, Robin wrote in the April 1977 issue of *The Voice*.

And in October of 1976 the GAE asked the CRTC to withhold CBH's license until "it adopted a non-discriminatory policy."

The request was denied. The CRTC renewed the station's licence with no mention of the GAE's intervention in February 1977.

▼

Censorship was in the air in the late 1970s and early 1980s, and gays and lesbians in Halifax and across the country were engaged in many a fight back.

Locally, in 1978, customs seized a shipment of books from Diana Press, a lesbian feminist publishing house based in California, en route to Halifax leftist bookstore and community hub Red Herring Cooperative Books. The scandalous titles included *Lesbian Lives*; *Lesbian Home Journal*; and *The Lavender Herring*—all collections of stories and essays previously published in *The Ladder*, the first nationally distributed lesbian magazine in the US. The list of censored titles also included *Yesterday's Lessons*, an autobiography of a working-class butch lesbian; *All Our Lives: A Women's Songbook*; *Class and Feminism*; and *Lesbianism and the Women's Movement*. When Red Herring Cooperative member Denise Roberge said to the customs officer: "You mean to tell me that books on lesbians aren't allowed into the country?" he replied, "That's exactly what I mean to tell you."

As a small bookstore, Tom Burns's Alternate Book Shop procured much of its stock from Toronto's Glad Day Bookshop and The Oscar Wilde Bookshop, which was an arm of the Mattachine Society in New York City. The stores would give Tom 25 percent off—a "family discount" of sorts. When the books, which had been sent from the Oscar Wilde shop, arrived at the Canadian border, customs wouldn't let them through because "the word homosexual [was] on them," Tom recalls. In 1979 several copies of the gay porn magazine *Honcho,* destined for The Alternate Book Shop, were held at the border due to their "immoral or indecent" content. Often, shipments would languish at the border for a few days and then customs would hand them over, Tom says.

"If you can't read your own writers—people who are writing about your own problems and despairs and joys—then you are not enjoying or understanding your culture as a whole, as a complete entity," says Jim MacSwain. He adds with impish glee, "My goodness—we even [had] our own porn!"

"Without communications, there can be no organized community," Robin told the *Dalhousie Gazette* in 1979. "Without an organized community, we have no defense against attacks upon ourselves or our community."

The GAE organized a public meeting on censorship on January 31, 1979. Speakers included Tom Burns, Alex Wilson of *The Body Politic* Collective, and Lynn Murphy, who was at that time a Dartmouth librarian. In her introductory remarks, the meeting's co-facilitator, GAE member Georgina Chambers, called censorship "an attempt to divide the gay community from organizing for our rights."

The meeting was held the day after a picket-cum-puppet show was held in front of the Canada Customs building on Hollis Street to protest the "growing climate of censorship in Nova Scotia, which GAE sees as a threat to the freedom of speech and expression of all Canadians." Demonstrators chanted "Public access to public media! End CBC discrimination!"; "We have a right to read what we like! Don't ban gay books!" and "Free *The Body Politic*! Drop the charges!" Several others performed a puppet show. The oversized cardboard puppets, created by Jim MacSwain, depicted a customs official, a CBC announcer, and an Ontario Provincial Police officer. The trio covered their ears, mouth, and eyes respectively, replicating the "see no evil, hear no evil, speak no evil" monkeys.

▼

On the evening of April 22, 1977, Chris Shepherd was enjoying a night with friends at the Jury Room bar in downtown Halifax and was halfway through a drink when the bartender told him that the establishment would not serve "people of your kind." That night, about a dozen men were thrown out of the lounge. The bar's manager reportedly told the men "just take your queens and get the fuck out of here."

Shepherd refused to leave. He and a friend were arrested and charged with being "drunk and disorderly in a public place," because, he says, they couldn't arrest them for simply being gay. The two spent the night in jail. The other men immediately contacted the GAE upon leaving the bar.

The incident garnered substantial media coverage, including in *The 4th Estate*, whose headline read "Gays Barred—Trial By Jury Room." In the article, Neil Gillis, the general manager of the bar, was quoted as calling the men "undesirables." He later told the paper, "They're so obvious it's pathetic.... Society hasn't accepted them and I certainly haven't. I think I'm

CENSORSHIP

How it concerns you....

In Canadian politics, other groups, such as trade unions, women, blacks, native people and students may find themselves gagged by the power of the police, the state and the mass media.

We're fighting back...

The Supreme Court of Canada will soon decide whether the Vancouver Sun has violated B.C. human rights legislation. The CRTC will rule on CBC's corporate license renewal, after having heard an Intervention by the Canadian Lesbian and Gay Rights Coalition. On February 14, Judge Sid Harris will announce his verdict in the Body Politic trial. The GAE and Red Herring intend to challenge Customs over our right to read what we choose.

Demonstration

The GAE will hold a picket to protest censorship on Tuesday, January 30 from 12 noon to 1 pm in front of the Ralston Bldg at 1557 Hollis St, which houses the offices of Canada Customs. A special theatrical presentation is planned to dramatise the issue. IF YOU VALUE YOUR FREEDOM OF SPEECH AND EXPRESSION, WE URGE YOU TO ATTEND. Picketters will meet at 11:30 at the Turret Gay Community Centre, 1588 Barrington St., 3rd floor.

Meeting

On Wednesday, January 31 at 7:30 pm there will be a public meeting at the Turret around the subject of censorship. We will have speakers representing the Body Politic and Red Herring, as well as music and dancing. Please come and bring your friends. Admission free.

For more information, contact:

Gay Alliance for Equality
P. O. Box 3611
Halifax South Postal Station
B3J 3K6

tel: 429-4294
also Gayline at 429-6969

Who's being censored?

November 1974 - The Vancouver Sun, B.C.'s largest circulation daily, refuses to carry a classified ad for the Gay Alliance Towards Equality, advertising its newspaper. A survey conducted by the Body Politic revealed that over 70% of Canadian dailies (including the Chronicle Herald/Mail Star) refuse to carry any ads for gay organizations.

January 7, 1977 - In response to a complaint by the Gay Alliance for Equality of Halifax, CBC Radio announces a policy of refusing to broadcast Public Service Announcements for homosexual organizations.

July 18, 1977 - Two members of Toronto's Gay Alliance Toward Equality are arrested for distributing posters announcing a dance and a march against Anita Bryant. Similar harassment of people posting gay notices has been reported in Montreal and Halifax.

December 30, 1977 - Police raid the offices of Canada's highly-respected gay journal, the Body Politic, in connection with an article on youth sexuality called "Men Loving Boys Loving Ken". Police remove 12 cartons of material, including financial records, subscription lists, manuscripts and personal mail. Charges are laid against three officers of Pink Triangle Press for the distribution of "obscene" material. The raid has been denounced by groups and individuals ranging from the Canadian Periodical Publishers Assoc. to the mayor of Toronto, John Sewell.

October 4, 1978 - A Canada Customs officer informs Red Herring Co-operative Books of Halifax that lesbian books are not allowed in Canada. The statement concerned a shipment of lesbian and feminist books from Diana Press in San Francisco. There is a long history of gay literature being prevented from entering Canada.

How does it concern you?

Individually, these events are disturbing enough. Together they form a pattern that is frightening, not just for the gay community, but for all Canadians who are concerned about the fundamental right of free speech. An attempt is being made to stifle the efforts of gay people to communicate with each other and with the broader community. Rights taken for granted by most Canadians are being systematically denied the gay minority. While the mass media flatly refuse to carry our notices, our own newspapers are threatened with extinction through police harassment and court costs. Customs is trying to choke off our communications with gays in other countries. Even the basic freedom to post notices is in question.

Without communications, there can be no organized community. Without an organized community, we have no defense against attacks upon ourselves or our community.

If this can happen to gay people, it can happen to everyone. With the well-publicised "swing to the right"

A GAE flyer (circa 1979) announcing a public meeting and demonstration to protest "the growing climate of censorship in Nova Scotia."

(JIM MACSWAIN COLLECTION)

probably speaking for the average straight person. How can you be sympathetic to those people?"

"Those people," however, made up a substantial proportion—40 to 60 percent—of the bar's patrons, according to a gay man named Bill who was quoted in the article in *The 4th Estate*. (Bill actually "emptied his glass on Gillis" after a tense back-and-forth that fateful night.) It was not the first time that the bar—which had recently been bought by former Saint Mary's football coach Al Keith—had discriminated against gays, or against those who were assumed to be gay. The manager had previously phoned the Gayline requesting that gay people not be referred to the bar, and staff once refused to serve a group of actors from Neptune Theatre because they were wearing makeup.

The night after Chris and his friends were refused service, Anne Fulton, Deborah Trask, Robin, and Jim returned to the Jury Room to "test their policy." Robin was wearing his signature "GAY RIGHTS NOW" button to make the situation abundantly clear. When the foursome reached the front of the line, the bouncer told them that the bar had "had trouble with 'your movement' last night" and that Robin and Jim wouldn't be let in. Anne later wrote in a letter that the door staff told the group they would admit the women, but specifically not the men, because "we know what they do."

"After a bit of an argument, he realized that lesbians were very much a part of the gay movement," Anne wrote, and all four were shut out.

Al Keith refused to meet with the GAE to discuss their concerns, "tersely" telling the Alliance, "I choose not to," Robin Metcalfe wrote in the *Body Politic*.

In a meeting with the Human Rights Commission (HRC) in late March, an HRC officer told GAE reps that although the commission couldn't take action against the Jury Room, it agreed that "this sort of thing shouldn't happen." George McCurdy, director of the commission, later denied that the officer had ever said such a thing, but told *The 4th Estate* that they were looking at the incident "even though it does not properly fall under the jurisdiction of the commission," given that sexual orientation had not yet been added to the Human Rights Act.

On April 30, thirty-five GAE members and sympathizers picketed the Jury Room. The picket was successful in diverting a "great many" customers from the Jury Room, Anne later wrote for *The Voice*.

It was also a fortuitous event for Lynn Murphy, who had not yet become a fixture in the LGB and feminist communities. At the time, she was dating a young male professor at Saint Mary's University. On Saturday night, he asked what she'd like to do. Lynn—who then identified as a straight ally—said, "Well (ahem), they're picketing the Jury Room tonight and I'd like to go down and picket with the gay people." Lord love him, says Lynn, he said yes.

The picket prompted Lynn to take out a membership in the Alliance and soon after she struck up her first relationship with a woman. She later served on the civil rights committee and on the executive of the GAE, including as chair.

"Oh, it was just great," she says of that time. "You'd feel kind of like we were at the forefront and helping make a new and different society."

Meanwhile, the Jury Room continued to discriminate against gay people.

One afternoon, GAE member and drag performer Randy Kennedy went to the lounge for a drink with friends, including his friend George. George, who was wearing a full face of foundation and Marlene Dietrich eyebrows, purposely sat with his back to the bar. Soon after the server brought them their drinks, the manager walked over and told the group they had to leave—that they didn't serve gays. If they didn't leave, he said, he would call the police.

Thoroughly perturbed, Randy returned later that night—this time in drag. Wearing a leopard-print dress with a "slit up to here" and high heels, he says, "the men were all over me, buying me drinks and this and that." This time, Randy was allowed to stay, and only left the bar to dodge the affections of an unknowing bouncer.

That June, another group of GAE members wearing "GAY RIGHTS NOW" buttons—including Mary Ann, Robin, Robert Stout, and Anne—returned to the bar and were told that they "could sit there all night but wouldn't be served." Consequently, the GAE called for a boycott of the bar, which, Robin wrote in *The Body Politic*, "received considerable community support and has succeeded in cutting substantially the number of customers."

Robin told *The 4th Estate* that the Jury Room incident was "the first of its proportion in the metro area in recent years."

Anne Fulton, who was at that time the chair of the GAE, told *The Body Politic* that the fight had considerably raised the profile of the city's gay and lesbian population. Even the CBC gave the GAE's Jury Room protest "excellent

Members of the GAE protest discrimnation outside the Jury Room in 1977.
(ROBIN METCALFE COLLECTION)

coverage," Anne wrote in *The Voice*, "which was nice, since we had so recently picketed them."

"There are many people in the city who know we have been discriminated against and that gay people have no protection in the Human Rights Act," Anne said in *The Body Politic*. "The first step to eliminating repression is to make our oppression known. The gay community in Halifax is more aware than ever that the GAE and APPLE and other groups and individuals will stand behind them and that we can fight for our rights."

▼

Cruising for sex remained a mainstay in gay male culture in Halifax in the mid-to-late 1970s. Randy Kennedy describes the cruising scene of the day as "festive." Randy, who grew up in Dartmouth, was introduced to cruising by someone he met in the bathrooms of the Woodlawn Mall, which he happened upon while shopping with his mother at age fourteen. Those stalls became his regular "haunt."

Before he was even old enough to drive a car, he would hitchhike over to Halifax to cruise.

"There would be, like, fifteen to twenty people walking around that one little triangle," he says of The Triangle cruising area. "Then you'd go up on the hill and there was a parade of cars driving around and around and around." There were more men still on the side of the hill; sometimes there would be twenty-five or thirty under the trees, says Randy. At night, Camp Hill Cemetery was awash with the shadows of primarily closeted men looking for a "booty call," says Randy.

Anthony Trask's introduction to The Triangle was through someone he met while attending Acadia University in Wolfville, NS. The friend took Anthony to Halifax and marched with him around The Triangle, he tells me.

Some people even cruised the downtown boardwalks and the boats docked there, says Anthony.

"The thing is, as a community you meet somebody and you might have a sexual encounter with them and then that's as far as it goes sexually, but then you become good friends and pals," says Anthony, who "met a lot of people" through cruising.

▼

The bars, the sidewalks, the public bathrooms: they were all sites of struggle in 1970s Halifax.

Sitting in Anthony Trask's studio in the Toronto heritage building–turned arts and culture hub, 401 Richmond, I ask the former GAE staffer if he was ever gay-bashed while living in Halifax. "Oh yeah," he responds. His answer is consistent with those of most of the gay men I interviewed for this book. "The threat of violence was the main problem," he adds. "You learn to run fast."

One night, Anthony was walking across the Halifax Common when five guys approached him. "Hey boy, give us a dollar," the men said, before hurling a bicycle at Anthony. The force knocked him over but he was able to run to the road and stop a passing car.

"They were freaking out in the car," he says. "I was a mess." Anthony went straight to the police station, where he gave a statement. The police never laid charges.

"I was just always afraid from then on," says Anthony.

The GAE minutes are filled with reports of gay-bashings, particularly at The Triangle. In 1977 one GAE member reported being attacked four times by the same group in one year. At that meeting Robin described a similar attack, possibly by the same people.

Robin had met a friend for pizza after a recent breakup. When he was later walking home alone, someone walked up beside him and asked for the time, then someone else punched him in the side of the head. When Robin turned around there were four attackers. Robin, who "didn't know how to fight," remembers swinging his bag around. He "came to in the back of a police car; they'd found me lying in the street."

Robin was concussed and needed stitches in his lip. (He still has a small half-moon scar on his temple.) The police drove him home and told him he shouldn't be walking in that area—his own neighbourhood.

Once he was home, Robin called his friend Jeanette, who he had been with earlier that night. She called the police, and Robin went down to the station to look through binders of headshots. "If this had happened to anybody else I would have headed a committee," he says. "But because it happened to me I didn't have the spirit to do it."

Randy Kennedy "only" got bashed once. He was coming home from playing chess at a friend's place when two men pulled him into an alley behind the Dresden Arms Hotel. One grabbed the back of Randy's head and dragged his face across the brick. Randy started to fight back. The other man punched him in the side of the face, and Randy grabbed his hand and bit it. Remembering what his brother had told him about fighting, Randy grabbed the other man's hand and broke his fingers. Then he took off.

The next day Randy's friend Barry came to his place. "My God, what happened to you?" he asked. Randy's face was covered in scabs.

But according to Chris Shepherd, some gays did bash back.

"A number of us had just gotten so fed up with the whole gay-bashing scene in the city that we just put the word out that anybody who was willing to and able to stand up and have a fight...let's get to it," says Chris, who describes himself as six-foot-five with "a big mouth to match."

At one point, Chris remembers, the police asked the GAE to name the "vigilantes" so they could "go after us, not the gay-bashers." The GAE did not oblige.

GAE minutes from the mid-to-late 1970s also contain discussions about "the lack of police co-operation with gay victims" and "police harassment of gays."

"Police were still discriminating against gay people," says Tom. "Still a lot of 'faggot' talk and that sort of nonsense." Police didn't believe victims of gay-bashings, he adds, or they didn't care.

At a 1975 general members meeting, someone referred to as D. Norton reported that at a meeting with Halifax Police, the police had told GAE reps that there was "no problem in police–gay relations at present."

In February 1978 eight men were arrested in the washrooms at a Halifax Woolco store and charged with "gross indecency," which (according to GAE minutes) carried a maximum sentence of five years in jail. The men's names and addresses were released by local and national media outlets. One of the accused, a public figure, was later hospitalized with self-inflicted gunshot wounds. Two more of the men went into psychiatric care following the publicity.

A GAE statement on the incident reads, in part, "GAE protests the sensationalism of the media and its lack of discretion in this case. It is unusual for an equivalent story of a heterosexual nature to receive national press coverage."

In 1979 GAE Chairperson Clyde Richardson wrote to *The Body Politic*, telling them that the group had received reports of "RCMP raids on private homes in the Atlantic provinces—two in the Halifax–Dartmouth area and one in Fredericton during August and September."

▼

Halifax's first known gay and lesbian march took place on October 10, 1977, as a grand finale for the first annual Atlantic Gay Conference. In those days, says Robin, "you always marched at a conference." And so, on that Monday in October, attendees took their demands for changes to the provincial Human Rights Act to the front lawn of Province House.

The conference, entitled "Our Atlantic Gay Community—United Against Oppression," had been held from October 8 to 10 at The Turret. Officially sponsored by the GAE and APPLE, the conference included workshops on coming out, feminism, Acadian gays, gays and Christian life, lesbian mothers, and developing a political strategy for gay rights.

"It was great for me," says Tom Burns. "The only time I had ever seen that many gay people before was at a dance in Montreal."

At the time there were those within the Halifax gay community who "were into celebrating the arched eyebrow; [who had] a camp sensibility which clashed with the perceived—and often actual—humourlessness of the left," Robin, who considers himself to be a lefty, says with a laugh.

The Atlantic conference seems to have brought the groups together. Robin recalls a picture of "the group of them [those who didn't particularly identify as being leftist or activist] standing proudly behind a banquet table because they had produced the food"—a beautiful meal for a conference of "chiefly lefty activist people."

"It's not like we were completely opposed to each other," he adds. "More than anything, it was a cultural difference."

Not even a year later, the GAE and APPLE hosted LGB folks from across the country for the sixth annual Conference for Lesbians and Gay Men. It was the "first Canada-wide conference to be held in the Atlantic region."

The annual National Gay Rights Coalition conferences were an opportunity for gay Canada "to talk to—and about—itself," *The Body Politic* wrote in

Mary Ann Mancini, Anne Fulton, and John Damien at the Atlantic Gay Conference, Halifax, October 1977. Damien was fired from his job with the Ontario Racing Commission because he was gay. **(ROBIN METCALFE COLLECTION)**

the lead-up to the conference. The conference took place in the context of "a developing crisis situation," the editorial continued. In 1977 former beauty queen, singer, and orange juice spokesperson Anita Bryant led a successful campaign to repeal a Florida ordinance prohibiting discrimination against LGB people in housing and employment. She then took her anti-gay campaign on the road, including to Toronto, Edmonton, and Moose Jaw, where she was met with large protests. Also part of the crisis, the *Body Politic* article argued: lesbians being fired from the army or losing custody of their children; John Damien's lawsuit against the Ontario Racing Commission, who fired him because he was gay; *The Body Politic* itself facing obscenity charges; and the fact that "freedom of expression is being attacked on a number of fronts."

And there was no rest for the (supposedly) wicked. Two weeks before the conference, the organizers found themselves without a venue. "A certain

Bob O'Neill during the protest that followed the Atlantic Gay Conference in October 1977. **(ROBIN METCALFE COLLECTION)**

Pickets went up at Saint Mary's University after the school abruptly cancelled the booking for the 1978 Conference for Lesbians and Gay Men. **(ROBIN METCALFE COLLECTION)**

rascal who worked at Saint Mary's had led us on to believe that we had it all booked," Robin explained at a 2SLG history panel organized by Pride Nova Scotia, the body representing 2SLGBTQIA+ government employees, in 2018. When that staff person left their position, Saint Mary's realized that an LGB conference had been booked on their campus, and withdrew the conference's booking. "So along with hustling with two weeks' notice to find a new venue, which was Dalhousie, we also had to organize a picket of Saint Mary's," says Robin, who was conference co-coordinator with Georgina Chambers.

"The Conference, subtitled 'The Fight Against Repression' appears to have its first example of such in the dispute over space now happening at Saint Mary's," the GAE's newsletter from that period reads.

The Saint Mary's picket would be life-changing for some. Barbara James, who had been born and raised in Halifax, was outed on the CBC news when she was captured on-camera at the SMU picket. "The news went around my family in about one hour post-broadcast, and that was that—Barbara was a lesbian," she wrote to me in an email.

The conference itself "was very stimulating, very exciting, and we had no clue of how groundbreaking it was," says Katherine MacNeil, who did some translation for the conference.

Between June 28 and July 3, conference-goers attended workshops conducted by an impressive lineup of speakers, including openly gay Metropolitan Community Church (MCC) Minister Brent Hawkes, on the topics of "Gays and the Church" and "Prisoners' Rights." *Body Politic* collective member and author of "Men Loving Boys Loving Men," Gerald Hannon, spoke on "Obscenity/Censorship." Toronto-based activist and *The Body Politic* writer Gary Kinsman, who would go on to help found Gays and Lesbians Against the Right Everywhere (GLARE) and the Lesbian and Gay Pride Day Committee of Toronto, presented on "Gays and Socialism." The conference also featured local talent: Anne Fulton presented on "Lesbian Power—A Strategy for the Movement," Nancy Brister (who was in her mid-thirties) spoke on the topic of "Older Lesbians," and APPLE members Ava Greenspun and Margo Pearce facilitated a workshop on "Anarcha-Feminism." Artist and so-called "cultural icon" Evergon facilitated "Gay Cultural Workers and Sissyhood." Workshops reflected issues that the LGB community was grappling with, including "Lesbian Mothers and Lesbians and Child Custody'; "Gay Fathers"; "Gays and the Police"; and "Youth Sexuality."

There was a lot of excitement around that conference "because there was a big influx of everybody, and everybody sort of getting off on just being together," says Anthony.

There was also a definite "sexual energy" at that conference, says Jim MacSwain, who was the conference's cultural coordinator. "When people came here there were definitely affairs and exchanges of liquids."

"I think for The Turret that was probably a turning point as well, because then we were on the map," says GAE member and future executive member Katherine MacNeil. "We got some press coverage and people got to know about us, and they saw that there were so many people who were not afraid to go out in public and march up and down the street." Post-conference, more people started coming to the club, she says.

"GAE attempted the most ambitious conference program to date: in the length of the conference, in the number of workshops, in the extent of the cultural activities and in the attempt at bilingualism," reads the report from the conference planning committee. Attendance, however, was "far below" the three to four hundred people expected, with a total of 142 delegates.

As Becki L. Ross notes in *The House That Jill Built: A Lesbian Nation in Formation,* the most contentious moment of the conference was when attendees voted to reverse a decision made at the 1977 Saskatoon conference to ensure "50 per cent of the decision making power for lesbians despite the fact that lesbians did not make up 50 per cent of the delegates" at future national conferences. Several of the Prairie delegates, who put the original motion forward, walked out. After the conference Weisa Kolansinka, a lesbian feminist from Saskatoon, wrote in *Prairie Woman* newspaper that "many prairie gay and lesbian delegates came away from the conference saddened, frustrated and angry."

There were two exceptions to the low attendance, said the conference planning committee report: for the play *The Night They Raided Truxx* and for the requisite march to Province House, which drew 150 people.

The Night They Raided Truxx, written by Paul Ledoux and Terry Last and directed by Rosemary Gilbert, sets the 1977 police raid of Montreal gay bar Truxx to music. Last had been in the bar—but had not been arrested—on the night of the raid. The Truxx raid led to the largest mass arrests at that time in Canada since the imposition of the War Measures Act during the FLQ crisis in Quebec in 1970. The bar's owner was found guilty of "keeping a common bawdy house," sentenced to ten days in jail, and given a five thousand dollar fine. Though most of the cast members were straight, as was Ledoux, the cast did include two well-known Halifax-based gay actors and current-day elders, Hugo Dann and Jim MacSwain. "I sang my little heart out," Jim remembers. Deborah Trask remembers a local queen teaching a couple of actors how to walk in heels, up and down the stairs at The Turret.

The bTheatrical Company's production played to two full houses and continued a "laughing to avoid the tears tradition," *Body Politic* collective member Ed Jackson wrote in *The Body Politic.*

One such number featured a "VD doctor" in Mae West drag "sashaying about the stage wielding a gigantic Q-tip tied with a bow," thrusting it towards the men. (The men arrested at Truxx were subjected to a mandatory VD test.) "The comic exaggeration of this moment was abruptly stopped when Ralph, the older man, refuses to submit to further humiliation. 'This has gone far enough,' he declares and strides off-stage," Jackson wrote.

"For a lot of the community in Halifax we knew nothing of what had happened in Montreal," says Katherine of the police raid. "So that was an education for us. It was kind of a harsh awakening, I guess you could say."

The show climaxed with a group number: "Gay Until The Day I Die," the title of which was also printed on pink balloons, two of which Robin has preserved in his archives. Jackson felt, however, that something was missing—something that could have "conveyed the spirit of the 2000-person demonstration" following the raid. "Nevertheless, *The Night They Raided Truxx* is a substantial advance for gay agitprop theatre in Canada," Jackson surmised.

The play about Truxx wasn't the only theatrical event on the agenda at that year's national conference; Jim MacSwain also debuted his one-person show, *The Bearded Lady's Reflection,* at The Turret.

Swathed in a flowing gown, Jim, as Bearded Lady, opened the show: "In ancient lands women with beards were worshipped, partaking of that prophetic mystery that blurs the distinction between the sexes.

"My sisters, those ripe women with their halos of hair were broken by the mobs of crazed priests who worshipped sexless abstractions of purity.... Come, bearded ladies, out of your caves; let this century have a good long stare," he proclaimed.

Jim—whom Robin Metcalfe described as "delightful as a magician, always charmingly, eccentrically, irrepressibly, gay" in a 1979 *Body Politic* article—had wanted to do something in drag without forsaking his beard. He also wanted to "portray a woman who was very strong in keeping her beard in spite of the pain and struggles of growing up in a repressive society," he told Robin. Fittingly, given that the play took place at a gay and lesbian conference, the bearded lady was also a lesbian.

For bisexual elder Lynn Murphy, talking about the national conference brings back memories of heartbreak. Lynn's girlfriend—her most serious lesbian relationship, still—broke up with her the night before the conference's closing march. "Oh my God, I cried all day, and I was driving the car, and I was not safe to be driving," Lynn told me. She had invited "all kinds of people" to come to her place for dinner that night. "Thank God she, at least, didn't come."

That November the GAE hosted the annual Atlantic gay and lesbian conference, that year entitled "Building A Community Spirit." The GAE's newsletter printed two responses the group received to its advertisements for

```
                                        The bTheatrical Company
                                               presents


 SPECIAL THANKS TO:                              THE

 N. S. Dept. of Education                       NIGHT
 Atlantic Institute of Education
 Video Theatre                               THEY RAIDED
 Seaweed Theatre
 N. S. College of Art and Design               TRUXX
 Neptune Theatre
 Mermaid Theatre
 Canadian Broadcasting Corporation
 Bob Shortt
 David Weir                            Written by:    Terry Last and Paul Ledoux

                                       Music by:      Sam Boskey

 A VERY, VERY SPECIAL THANKS TO THE    Choreography by:  Sekai
 MEMBERS AND MANAGEMENT OF THE GAY
 ALLIANCE FOR EQUALITY AND THE TURRET.
 WITHOUT THEIR HELP, CO-OPERATION AND
 UNDERSTANDING THIS PRODUCTION WOULD
 NOT HAVE BEEN POSSIBLE.               DIRECTED BY:   Rosemary Gilbert Weir


                          1978
```

The program for *The Night They Raided Truxx*, which was performed during the sixth annual Conference for Lesbians and Gay Men in 1978. **(JIM MACSWAIN COLLECTION)**

the conference. The first, scrawled on a poster for the conference, got straight to the point: "Christ has condemned and destroyed your kind. Read your Bible, scum-of-the-earth, molesters of innocent children, agents of Satan, cursed by God and damned forever."

The second, signed by "Straight Joe," who identified as a cured homosexual, said that the GAE's plan to build a community spirit was "bound for failure." (At the time, the GAE's membership was a thousand people strong.)

"And the word 'Gay' is not appropriate. Let's...use the right words 'sex deviates,'" the letter continued. "When God told people to be fruitful and multiply, he did not mean two women or two men. All that can multiply is the devil's work."

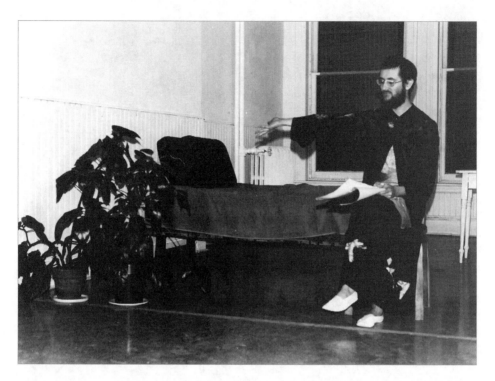

Jim MacSwain performing his one-person show, *The Bearded Lady's Reflection*, at The Turret during the sixth annual Conference for Lesbians and Gay Men in 1978.
(JIM MACSWAIN COLLECTION)

During the opening of the conference, then-chair Clyde Richardson lifted the defaced poster high into the air, letting it sail "through the air and onto the floor, where it belongs," Glenn Walton wrote in the GAE's newsletter *Have You Heard.*

▼

Deborah Trask was born in Montreal to two Maritimers and migrated back east in 1968 to attend Acadia University. In 1972 she moved to Halifax, and by November of that year she had secured herself a good government job.

"I started off using 'gay' because we were all gay, but quickly made that distinction," and it was always "lesbian" after that, she says.

According to Deborah, who got involved in the GAE in 1976, there weren't "many women who wanted to come and sit through meetings" where there was a "fair bit of squabbling." It didn't help that the group was predominantly men. Deborah, who would later get involved in the Second Story Women's Centre in Lunenburg County, the Council of the Women's Action Coalition (WAC/NS), and National Action Committee on the Status of Women, points to systemic reasons more women were not involved in GAE. Women had only recently started earning a minimum wage equal to a man's, and many lesbians had a limited income and had children. Tellingly, the GAE didn't include "lesbian" in its name until 1988.

Deborah's involvement in the GAE drew ire from some lesbians. One day a delegation of lesbians showed up at her house, which she was sharing with her "baby brother," Anthony Trask. The women read Deborah the riot act—"all these things I had done that were in contravention of what a real lesbian should be." (One of the women later apologized to Deborah for her role in the house visit.) It's not surprising, then, that Deborah didn't feel "any support from the broader gay community" for the many years she put into GAE.

GAE's membership was also largely white.

In the 1970s Walter Borden—who identifies as gay Africadian/Mi'kmaw—was working for the Black United Front (BUF), with the Black Inmates Association, and performing on the stage at Neptune Theatre. In 1974, Walter began writing his one-man show *Tightrope Time: Ain't Nuthin' More Than Some Itty Bitty Madness Between Twilight & Dawn*, which he recently re-launched at The Bus Stop Theatre in Halifax.

"We just didn't have time for [the GAE] because we're dealing with something else here," he says of his fellow Black activists. "Unless something was really defined and profound, you just didn't have time to deal with it." After a decade or so at the centre of the province's Black civil rights movement, Walter didn't feel as if the local gay movement was radical enough. "If it was something like Stonewall, yeah, that's what I'm talking about," he told me in 2016.

Chris Shepherd, who first got involved in the GAE in 1976, says there were only a "handful" of Black folks within the Alliance. He would go on to be elected GAE's treasurer in 1980. "I've never let my race be any issue," says Chris. "If I want to go somewhere, I'm goin'. If I want to do something, I'm doin', and be damned if you don't like it."

Faith Nolan, who is of mixed African, Mi'kmaw, and Irish heritage, remembers the GAE as being mostly white middle-class guys. "And the white guys that I hung around with were pretty working class because I washed dishes. We weren't the intelligentsia," she says with a laugh.

Lorne Izzard first learned of the GAE through two other Amherst expats, Clairemarie Haley and Ed Thibodeau, who were active within the Alliance. "I found it to be a bit disorganized and very white," says Lorne.

Walter agrees. "There was such infighting and such foolishness," he says of the GAE (and its successor, the Gay and Lesbian Association, or GALA).

According to Lynn, the meetings would get pretty tense. In reading through past GAE minutes, I could clearly see lines drawn amongst the membership: who moved and seconded motions, who nominated whom for elected positions, who signed onto what petition or open letter. "Some people were probably a little bit miffed by the activism that we brought into the meetings," says Jim MacSwain.

"It's easy to romanticize in retrospect, but being in community didn't mean we didn't scream and yell at each other and have horrible fights," says Robin Metcalfe. When Robin attended *Body Politic* meetings in Toronto he knew that the folks there were quarrelling because they would talk in hushed tones. But it wasn't like that back home. "They'd stomp out, they'd threaten lawsuits, they'd burst out in tears—it was quite dramatic. Then we'd meet again next week."

In his 1978 letter of resignation as GAE chairperson, Robin wrote: "We must strive to be more mature and cautious in our dealings with one another. It is very easy to split up into cliques and factions, and to see those who differ from us as enemies. We must remember that the vast majority of people in the GAE are not enemies, but potential allies with whom we may differ in ideas and viewpoint.

"It is important to reach out to one another, to listen to and respect one another, in order to build a real community of mutual support. We need that community because, out in the broader world, we have real enemies who would rob us of all our rights as human beings and who are presently organizing to do just that."

"I've had conflict with lots of lesbians, and I've had conflict with lots of gay guys too...over this tiny little space that we could be in," lesbian feminist activist Diann Graham told me. "But as the laws changed, and as we found that we were protected—you know, in our relationships, in our housing, in our parenting—as all those laws changed, I find the conflicts in the community lessened."

Chapter 4

LEAPING LESBIANS: VOICES OF WOMEN

(1970s)

In 1972, Nancy Brister was living in Halifax, "trying desperately to meet some women, and I couldn't," she tells me over the phone. When she joined the Brenton Street Women's Centre, Nancy thought: "Aha! This is where I'm going to meet all types of lesbians." But she didn't meet one. "I just wanted to be with my own kind," she tells me. "It's a pretty lonely life if you can't identify with people, you know." Her disappointment prompted Nancy—who still "wasn't really out"—to book the women's centre on Friday nights for a lesbian drop-in. The house, Nancy remembers, was owned by a gay male lawyer. Nancy spent several Friday nights sitting in the centre alone before other women started to hear about the drop-in. Finally, a few lesbians dropped by. "That was nice; it was nice to have a place," Nancy says.

Back then, most people in the community were younger than she was, says Nancy, who was born in 1941. Though she didn't have any elders per se, there was one lesbian couple of women her age who had been out for ten years when she met them. Those women acted as mentors, taking her under their wing. "They protected me, tried to show me the way."

Newly divorced, one of Nancy's biggest fears was that if her husband found out she was a lesbian he would take her son.

"I...lived for probably four years with the fear," she says.

When he did find out, Nancy says, he simply said, "Oh, that's interesting."

Her fear was rooted in reality. In 1974 a Saskatoon lesbian, Darlene Case, had lost custody of her two children to her ex-husband because she was a lesbian. It was a precedent-setting case. According to a 1976 *Body Politic* article, each year hundreds of lesbian mothers across the country lost their children; some made it to court, others didn't. Judges were known to be particularly hostile towards lesbian activists.

"Lesbians are Mothers Too," reads an unattributed and undated handout in the National Gay Rights Coalition (NGRC) folder at the Nova Scotia Archives. It states that even those "who have managed to obtain divorces and custody of their children live under the constant threat of exposure, of being declared unfit mothers solely because they are lesbians." The handout appealed to gay men to support their lesbian sisters and prioritize child custody in the fight for gay liberation.

In 1978, members of a group called Wages Due Lesbians—a Toronto-based Marxist-feminist group that that drew attention to women's unpaid domestic labour—established the Lesbian Mothers Defence Fund. The group offered "pre-legal advice and information on custody battles in Canada and the United States, as well as referrals to lawyers, financial assistance, and peer counselling" until 1987.

"Some of the husbands and partners were fine with it and they had a good friendly connection, and other ones were not, and so they lost the children," says Sandra Nimmo, who is a lesbian mother herself. Sandra remembers riding on the back of another lesbian's motorcycle to the South Shore to visit that woman's children, who were living with their father. On the way home, Sandra could feel the woman's tears falling on her hands. "I'm thinking, 'Oh God, I hope she can see." When she came out and separated from her husband in the late 1970s, Sandra's priority was making sure that her three children (who moved with her from Dartmouth to Halifax) were settled, and that life was as "normal for them as I could make it." She was careful that there wasn't anything too blatantly gay or lesbian in the house "that would make people feel that this was unusual for the kids," she tells me. "I had to be mindful of all of that, so my life was taken up a lot with that."

Sandra's divorce and child custody battle took a total of eight years. Every August she got a notice that they were going to court again. In the end, Sandra was the first lesbian in Nova Scotia to gain full (not shared) custody of her children. Sandra and her partner would often have lesbian friends over for brunch, and her kids would be exposed to these "really wonderful women" she says. "When they got in their teens, they couldn't figure out—why are people so against gays and lesbians?"

▼

Finding your people, Nancy tells me, is the first step. "Then, depending on how comfortable you are with your group—and I was, totally—it gives you the strength to say, 'To heck with the world. I am going to march in that march, and I am going to come out to my mother.'"

The year 1975 was declared International Women's Year by the United Nations, and as lesbian feminist activist, Diann Graham, writes in *And I Will Paint the Sky: Women Speak the Story of Their Lives*, "it was a time which brought about changes in mindset and policy which have affected every aspect of our present society."

That year, the local chapter of socialist group In Struggle organized Halifax's first International Women's Day celebrations at Veith House, a historic house and community hub in north end Halifax.

Carol Millet was going to Mount Saint Vincent University when she found In Struggle. The Halifax cell of the group was primarily focused on galvanizing support for workers, unions, and their various strikes—in particular, the Canadian Union of Postal Workers, who Carol remembers as being "very militant" back then. Members would visit picket lines and hand out their Marxist-Leninist newspaper and stage street theatre in order to spread their propaganda.

In Struggle was being monitored by the police, Carol remembers, and the Halifax cell was infiltrated. The police had taken photos of the members and knew who each one was, but blew their own cover when the "plant" tried to strike up a relationship with Carol—the only out lesbian (or gay person) in the group at the time.

"So he didn't get very far, which was good," Carol recounts with a laugh. "We did have a good chuckle about that."

Women within In Struggle continued to organize IWD until 1978 when, according to *Groups Dynamic: A Collection of Nova Scotia Her-Stories* (a 1990 booklet documenting various facets of women's "herstory" in Nova Scotia), "there was a shift of emphasis from trade unionism to feminism" and the organizing began to take place at a women's centre known as "A Woman's Place'" at the YWCA's Forrest House. The YWCA-owned Victorian building, located at 1225 Barrington Street, had been rehabilitated in 1977 by a group of YW volunteers, including Alexa McDonough (who would be elected leader of the Nova Scotia New Democratic Party in 1980).

Brenda Bryan, originally from North Sydney, moved to Halifax in 1968 to attend the Nova Scotia College of Art and Design (NSCAD) at age sixteen. Brenda met her first girlfriend at NSCAD and was introduced to an American lesbian separatist collective known as The Furies by one of her professors. "On the hunt" for the local women's movement, Brenda discovered that the high-rise where she and her girlfriend lived was directly across the street from the Brenton Street Women's Centre.

Brenda worked on both of peace activist and NDP candidate Muriel Duckworth's campaigns for a seat in the Nova Scotia Legislature, where she met Alexa McDonough. She worked with Alexa and a "host of other women" to renovate and open Forrest House.

It was an exciting time, "because half the time, you know, we were in back rooms and back alleyways," says Brenda. "We didn't have the money. To have the Y putting together programs for the betterment of women...was a huge step up."

"A Woman's Place identifies with women's needs in order that they might fully participate in their new role in society today," reads an undated leaflet. "The new role or fourth dimension portrays woman as a person herself using her abilities in a changing world in contrast to the three dimensional role of woman as wife, mother and housewife, an essentially passive and dependent role in a timeless world."

A Woman's Place was a space, according to the pamphlet, for women to "meet on their own terms; to have fun, to learn from each other, and develop together."

Forrest House was home to various women's organizations and offered women-only workshops on feminism, assertiveness, coping with being single again, sexuality, "one nighters," math anxiety, budgeting, getting to know your car, self-defence, domestic violence, rape counselling, women in politics, and more. It produced a calendar of events, the feminist Facebook of its day, as well as the *Women's Words* newsletter. In 1979 A Woman's Place sent a letter to Joe Clark advocating for the removal of the sections of the Indian Act that discriminated against women.

A Woman's Place housed groups such as Women's Employment Outreach (WEO) and had a living room, dining room, and small kitchen. According to Diane Guilbault, from 1979 to 1980 Forrest House ran a rape crisis line staffed entirely by volunteers.

By the time Forrest House was up and running, Brenda was living in a Bishop Street housing co-op that the members referred to as "Dyke Motor Inn." Because the "Inn" was close to Forrest House, it became a safe haven for lesbians who were unsure about A Woman's Place.

Lynn Murphy—who sat on Forrest House's health and social action committees—remembers being told there was "too much obvious lesbian activity" at the house. "They didn't mean that people were having sex in the bathroom," she says, but there was too much "lesbian talk" and women dancing together at the women-only dances.

Straight feminists, says Brenda, felt that "the lesbians were damaging the women's movement."

"I thought [that] was hilarious because there wouldn't have been anywhere near the women's movement if the lesbians hadn't stepped in," she says.

Fearful of being labelled "man-hating feminists," some 1970s women's organizations eagerly distanced themselves from lesbians, whom Betty Friedan (author of *The Feminine Mystique*) famously dubbed "the lavender menace."

"We all left, and they had not realized how many of us there were," Lynn says. *Groups Dynamic* notes that in 1979 the International Women's Day dance was held at The Turret, "owing to ill feeling about objections raised the previous year at the YWCA about lesbians dancing together."

Brenda guesses that about 80 percent of the women keeping Forrest House afloat were lesbians, but they weren't all out to the same extent. "Some of those women that were hanging out at the women's centre were married with kids."

A few weeks on "somebody came to one of the well-known lesbian participants and asked us to come back and we did," Lynn says. "Because where were we going to go?" she says with a laugh.

Abortion was one issue that brought straight and LB2S women together. Barbara James was one of the founding members of the Abortion Information and Referral Service (AIRS) in the late 1970s. "Access to abortion in the Atlantic Provinces was extremely limited at the time, and even where it was available, it was often down to the whim/political perspective of the doctor whether a woman was given access to services," Barbara told me in an email. "AIRS was a pretty limited service, but we tried to improve access to abortion to women outside metropolitan Halifax. With virtually no budget, it's amazing that we reached anyone, but I remember calls received and access offered to women in Newfoundland, Cape Breton, and Prince Edward Island."

From 1978 to the early 1980s Sandra Nimmo was one of two staffers at Forrest House, and, in fact, it was her first job. At thirty-one, Sandra had come out as lesbian and separated from her husband of ten years. She was "a bit older" and had never worked outside the house. When she went back to Dalhousie University to complete her degree in music education, Sandra was able to place her three children in daycare and work part-time as a counsellor at the centre.

Forrest House existed before Halifax had women's shelters. (In fact, Forrest House was part of the committee of groups that later founded Bryony House, a shelter for abused women and their children, and Sandra sat on its board). "I remember one particular woman who had run away from her abusive relationship," Sandra says. She had travelled across Canada by train and had arrived at Forrest House in need of a place to stay. "We had nothing but to give her a hotel room."

Because she was the only lesbian working in the house, Sandra also was the point person for other lesbians who came in, which was fine with her. Women who had just broken up with female partners often just needed to have somewhere to talk that felt safe, says Sandra.

By the time Diann Graham was working for Women's Employment Outreach (WEO) on the second floor, there was good lesbian visibility, and even drop-ins at Forrest House.

One woman, simply identified as "KD" in *We Dreamed of Another Way of Being,* the report that came out of the 2014 Lesbian Memory Keepers Workshop which brought lesbian women together to discuss and record lesbian history, recalls finding the book *Our Right To Love* in the Forrest House Library. "One day I came in, and I had rehearsed this in my house," she told the group. "I told the women I was a lesbian. And they pointed to the top of the stairs and said 'see Diann Graham.'"

▼

The first Halifax Reclaim the Night event—a feminist mainstay to this day—was organized by the Anarcha-Feminist group in October 1978 to "increase people's awareness that women aren't able to walk safely alone at night," organizer Diana Pepall told the *Dalhousie Gazette*. This puts Halifax squarely in step with the Take Back the Night marches held in Vancouver and in Ottawa, both in August of that year.

The Halifax march sprang from a discussion around an article in *Spare Rib* magazine about women "reclaiming the night" in Britain. Anarcha-Feminist group member Susan Holmes tells me that the group was aware of sexual assault allegations swirling around former "esteemed Premier," Gerald Regan, and was looking for a way for survivors to have a voice outside of the flawed legal system.

Susan, who was born in the Prairies and grew up in Quebec, moved to Nova Scotia to finish her first degree at Acadia University. She was married and a parent when she helped to start a feminist peer-counselling group after attending a talk from a visiting feminist therapist.

"That was a whole turning point of my life," Susan says. "I fell in love with one of the women in the group, surprised the hell out of myself, changed my whole life." It was 1975 and she was thirty.

Due to their "rejection of authority," Reclaim the Night organizers refused to ask for a permit for the march. (Thirty years later, the organizers of the Dyke and Trans March—of which I was a founding organizer—unknowingly followed this in these footsteps, also refusing to ask for a permit to march.)

"We made some very clear choices about that—we weren't going to tell the cops," Susan tells me in a cafe in Ottawa, where she lives now, "because the cops were never there when women needed help."

"The first Reclaim the Night march was such a big deal because it could not and it did not involve men," says organizer Meredith Bell. The reason, march organizers Diann Graham, Diane Guilbault, and Verona Singer wrote in *Groups Dynamic*, was that "our purpose is to empower women and act as a symbol of women's right to safety without male protection."

"Husbands need not apply, boyfriends need not apply," Meredith continues. "Organize your shit…and do something supportive of this, and get the hecklers off the street. Like, why should we have to do that?" So male allies organized childcare, and later walked beside the march to deal with drunk and pissed-off male onlookers, and even went into the bars to conduct impromptu education over beer, says Susan.

The march started in the late evening on a Friday at Red Herring Cooperative Books and included between fifty and one hundred women, including reps from the International Socialists, Communists, and In Struggle—despite the fact that many of the march's posters had been torn down almost as soon as they went up. That first Reclaim the Night took little planning, says Susan.

Chanting, "We want streets without creeps!" the march made its way up Hollis, Inglis, and Queen Streets, along University Avenue and South Park Street (where a beer bottle was thrown from an apartment building), and down Spring Garden Road to Barrington Street. In "A Personal View: Women Reclaim the Night," printed in Halifax-based lesbian newsletter *The Sisters' Lightship*, Ruth Holden-Bingham writes of enjoying "screaming at the top of my lungs" while clutching a bright red-lettered placard that read "See me—not my body." According to the *Dalhousie Gazette*, some women at the back of the march reported being followed and harassed.

That first march, Ruth writes, ended back where it all started, at Red Herring, where the women discussed self-defence classes.

"I just remember walking down there with all my friends around me…in the middle of the street, not on the sidewalk. Knowing that the cops were really irritated by us, and thinking that was just fine," Susan says of that first march.

"For me it was all celebratory," she continues. "Celebratory of women's power and independence."

▼

But not everyone was able to take to the streets during the later half of the seventies.

An early Reclaim the Night march in Halifax. **(DIANN GRAHAM COLLECTION)**

In 1975, twenty-four-year-old Darl Wood joined the military. Originally from Truro, she had left her hometown in 1968, oscillating between Halifax and Toronto. Darl, who didn't identify as a lesbian when she enrolled, met her first love in the Forces. Even after falling for another woman, a reservist, Darl says she doesn't know if she was aware of the term "lesbian." It was an "intense" relationship, she says. "But then, relationships in the military were very intense," she adds, noting the almost-instantaneous friendships she developed. "Because you never knew when someone was going to be stationed across the world. You just made the most of that."

Darl developed close-knit friendships with other women, some of them lesbians, in the military. It was almost like a secret society, she says. They met through softball and volleyball. Sports were big in the military, especially for lesbians, says Darl, because you got to travel to different bases and meet other women. Spending time with other women in the same situation was really nice, and they knew how to throw a good party.

Darl says that while she was in the military she wasn't "really aware of any political movement that was happening." She didn't go to Thee Klub or The Turret.

"What I was aware of was Martina Navratilova," she adds with a laugh, referring to the tennis player who would later come out as a lesbian.

Lesbian feminist activist and Rumours manager Brenda Bryan. **(ANNE FULTON)**

Anthony Trask in 1977. Anthony had shaved off his beard just before taking this photo to mail to a friend. **(ANTHONY TRASK COLLECTION)**

Darl Wood with her mentor and Voice of Women Nova Scotia founder, Muriel Duckworth. **(ANITALOUISE MARTINEZ)**

Deborah Trask. **(ROBIN METCALFE COLLECTION)**

Marchers at International Women's Day 1981. Brenda Bryan is at left holding the banner. Jackie Barkley is centre left holding the megaphone. **(DIANN GRAHAM)**

Early 1980s beachgoers at the annual "gay picnic" at Silver Sands beach in Cow Bay, NS, sunbathing by a pink triangle flag. **(JIM DEYOUNG COLLECTION)**

Chris Shepherd in summer of 1981 at Silver Sands beach in Cow Bay for the first annual "gay picnic." **(JIM DEYOUNG COLLECTION)**

Randy Kennedy at Silver Sands beach in Cow Bay for the annual "gay picnic" in the early 1980s. **(JIM DEYOUNG COLLECTION)**

Lorne Izzard. **(JIM DEYOUNG COLLECTION)**

GAE member and Turret staff person Reg Giles holding the flag of Fredericton Lesbians and Gays (FLAG) in front of the Turret logo. **(JIM DEYOUNG COLLECTION)**

From left, K Tetlock, Chris Parsons, Meredith Bell, and Diane Guilbault. Diane is wearing a "Women Reclaim the Night" button with a pink triangle. **(MEREDITH BELL COLLECTION)**

A group of protestors that includes Mary Ann Mancini, Debbie Pye, Bob Stout, Wendell Enman, David Ayotte, Tom Burns, Bob O'Neill, Robin Metcalfe, and Dene Roach at Province House after the first (known) LGB march, which closed out the 1977 Atlantic Gay Conference. **(ROBIN METCALFE COLLECTION)**

Mary Ann Mancini at Halifax's first (known) LGB picket, which was on February 17, 1977, against CBC Radio when management refused to run a Gayline public service announcement. **(ROBIN METCALFE COLLECTION)**

Alexa McDonough (left), the newly elected the leader of Nova Scotia's New Democratic Party, and Lynn Murphy at The Turret in 1981. **(ROBIN METCALFE COLLECTION)**

GAE founding member and lesbian activist Anne Fulton. **(ROBIN METCALFE COLLECTION)**

Robin Metcalfe and Jim MacSwain at the October 1977 Atlantic Gay Conference. **(ROBIN METCALFE COLLECTION)**

Bisexual feminist activist Lynn Murphy (right) at an International Women's Day rally in 1981. Jackie Barkley is at centre holding the megaphone. **(DIANN GRAHAM)**

Randy Kennedy in drag as Lily Champagne.
(RANDY KENNEDY COLLECTION)

This march was held during a national gay and lesbian conference in Halifax in 1978.
(ROBIN METCALFE COLLECTION)

Officially, gay men and lesbians were not permitted to serve in the Canadian Armed Forces. As Gary Kinsman and Patrizia Gentile write in *The Canadian War on Queers: National Security as Sexual Regulation,* "regardless of the 1969 reform, state bodies and the RCMP continued to view gay men and lesbians as security risks who were suffering from a character weakness." In other words, 2SLGBQ people had a shameful secret and were especially vulnerable to blackmail, which could put national security in jeopardy. In fact, before 1976, when the language in the administrative order prohibiting 2SLGBQ folks from serving was updated, it read that they did "not allow the retention of sex deviates in the Forces."

People suspected of being homosexuals were surveilled, interrogated, released, and labelled "not advantageously employable." According to Kinsman and Gentile, in the early 1970s there was an investigation into homosexual activity at RCAF Base Shearwater, outside of Halifax, which resulted in fifteen women being purged from the military. The higher-ups found out about those women from another young woman who was struggling with her own sexuality and had attempted suicide. "They took advantage of her. They truly did; they tortured her," a woman named Sue told Kinsman and Gentile.

The thing about the military, says Darl, is that "your training or your conditioning is like a cult. Your whole life is encapsulated in the military; that becomes your whole life. So you eat, drink, and sleep it, right?

"So when you're under pressure that this might be taken away from you, you become very secretive and you have to watch everything you do and say," she says. Darl's phone was tapped and she knows of other people who were followed.

To this day, Darl does not know how the military found out she was a lesbian. "It was very traumatic; it was like always looking over your shoulder, always being aware that at any time or point in your career it could be cut short and that you could be interrogated," says Darl. "And that's what happened to me."

The Special Investigation Unit (SIU) took Darl into custody. According to the statement Darl gave at the 2015 press conference for the We Demand an Apology Network, a group formed to force the federal government apologize for what is now known as the "gay purge," the SIU members brought her into a small room where she was interrogated for "hours and hours." Two men grilled Darl about her sex life. "They wanted to know how, who, when, where, and what we did in the privacy of our home and bedroom," Darl said in 2015. "The worst part is that it took me years to realize what happened to me was a sexual assault," she says of the interrogation. The men also tried to get Darl to disclose the names of other lesbians in the Forces; everyone who was interrogated was under enormous pressure to do the same.

Darl was discharged from the armed forces in 1978, just three years after she joined. It was three months between the time of her interrogation and her official release, and "to add insult to injury they were busy at the release centre so I had to type up my own release form," she says.

Her release marked both the end of her career in the military and her relationship. Darl describes the next two years as "being in a catatonic state." She was devastated.

▼

On the Victoria Day weekend in 1976 Anne Fulton drove what she called her "gorgeous hunk of rotting metal" to Kingston, Ontario, for a conference called "The Not-So-Invisible Woman: Lesbian Perspectives in the Gay Movement," which was held by the Queen's University Homophile Association. The conference—open to men and women—attracted approximately fifty men and forty-five women, though at least one feminist group refused to attend on account of the men's involvement.

"So the conference had an unexpected twist," Anne wrote. "The dykes took the conference into their own hands, and it began to focus seriously around the theory of dyke separatism...and the need for an autonomous lesbian organization within the country. We'd all grown tired of working behind the shadow of the men, of fighting for their aims and of not having the guts and self-confidence to fight for, let alone recognize, what we wanted."

Anne, the sole GAE delegate and one of only four attendees from outside Ontario, wrote about the conference—for which she was late, not an uncommon occurrence—for *The Voice*.

"From the moment that we women were alone, we wanted the rest of the conference to be mostly segregated," Anne wrote. "We felt that we had a great many things to discuss that did not concern the men."

Anne had never felt such "a strong common bond" with any group of people as she had with the out and proud conference "dykes."

The conference produced an official statement, which Anne included in her article in *The Voice*. It read in part: "We realize the need to build our power as lesbian women so that we need no longer subordinate our interests to those of the straight women or the men...straight or gay; and so that our lesbian sisters who are in the majority of cases still invisible to us, will have the possibility of coming out."

The Kingston conference led to two subsequent conferences, one in Toronto that summer, and one in Ottawa in fall 1976.

Members of Nancy Brister's consciousness-raising group also carpooled to lesbian conferences in Ontario and Quebec. It was at the registration table for one such conference that Nancy learned of Maggie's Farm—a women's collective farm just outside Tatamagouche, Nova Scotia, founded by two back-to-the-landers from Berkeley, California. After the conference, two or three of them went to meet the five women that made up Maggie's Farm.

Soon after, Nancy bought the house next door to the "picture perfect" farm. The women of Maggie's had originally invited Nancy and her partner to live with them, but at that point the small one-hundred-year-old farmhouse was already home to five women and four children.

Upon returning from the Kingston conference, Anne found that she couldn't work as enthusiastically with the men within GAE given their "somewhat different" objectives. She brought together a group of women in the hope of starting an autonomous lesbian organization back home, and APPLE—the Atlantic Provinces Political Lesbians for Equality—"blossomed." According to an editorial in the first and only issue of *The Sisters' Lightship*, a lesbian newsletter published in December 1978, APPLE was made up of women who represented "such a wide variety of backgrounds, philosophies, and experiences that we must conclude at times that our only common base is our membership in APPLE."

Post–Ottawa conference, APPLE got to work producing a new bilingual national lesbian journal, *LesbianCanadaLesbienne*, which Anne had committed to publishing at the conference; it would be printed on the coveted Gestetner at the MOVE offices.

The chapter about APPLE in *Groups Dynamic* ends with this author's note: "I'm sad and outraged that I must remain nameless until sexual orientation is included in provincial and federal human rights legislation and I am protected

The station wagon belonging to Maggie's Farm, a women's collective farm located outside Tatamagouche, Nova Scotia. **(ANNE FULTON COLLECTION)**

against discrimination." It seems clear to anyone who knew Anne that she was the author of this piece.

"She was so soft, she was so gentle, and nothing stopped her," Susan Holmes says, of Anne.

Meetings took place at the MOVE offices, Forrest House, The Turret, Red Herring, and in various members' living rooms and bedrooms. According to *Groups Dynamic*, APPLE boasted twenty-ish members who marched under the APPLE banner at IWD and Reclaim the Night marches. They raised funds with women's dances at The Turret and by selling baked goods made with apples, using the money to rent a van so they could drive to a conference in Toronto. They helped co-plan and facilitate workshops for the national gay and lesbian conference that was held in Halifax in 1979.

In December 1978 some of the women involved in APPLE had another go at creating a lesbian newsletter with *The Sisters' Lightship*. It featured a first-hand account by an APPLE member who attended the third annual Michigan Womyn's Music Festival (featuring African-American a cappella group Sweet Honey in the Rock), a personal account of the first Reclaim the Night, and an article on two APPLE-run "coffee houses." The coffee houses, which were informal gatherings held in October and November, included a rendition of the song "Bread and Roses" by lesbian feminist organizer Georgina Chambers; blues, spiritual, and calypso music from African, Mi'kmaw, and Irish musician and activist Faith Nolan; a set of folk and Scottish ballads by Anne Fulton; poetry; and a short feminist film by the women's media collective Reel Life.

Faith Nolan also played both originals and covers—she loved Odetta, Joan Baez, Woody Guthrie, Bessie Smith, and Billie Holiday—at The Turret and Ginger's, a local watering hole frequented by leftist activists, where her uncle Jimmy worked. Meredith Bell also remembers playing coffee houses at Odin's Eye on Argyle Street.

Faith remembers being the only woman of colour at the coffee houses. "I certainly didn't feel like I was totally welcomed or fit in," she says. "I have always just—if I wanted to go someplace, I would go there. I certainly insist upon my right to be wherever I want." She likens those socials to Three of Cups, a "lesbian feminist, almost separatist" coffee house she frequented in Toronto. She also remembers the good food—the falafels especially.

Faith was fourteen when she told her mother that she was queer, and was promptly kicked out of her home in Toronto. As Faith wrote in her essay for the 2017 anthology *Any Other Way: How Toronto Got Queer*, "At that time, in the queer community, we would help each other out, like Black people. There really weren't community organizations, so people took care of each other. If there was a young homeless queer, somebody would put them up." And so in 1971 she moved in with a trans woman named Dee Dee she had met at Toronto bar Momma Cooper's.

In 1976, at age nineteen, Faith returned to the city of her birth—Halifax. Faith, whose family hailed from Glace Bay, Sydney, and Africville, lived in the Nova Scotia Home for Colored Children—an orphanage for African-Nova Scotian children—until she was four years old.

When she arrived, Faith crashed with a gay man she worked with washing dishes at Frank's Restaurant. "I think we became family because, you know, we had our families turned against us, I suppose," she says.

It felt like there were only thirty lesbians in the city, says Faith. She met those women at house parities, at Deborah Trask's, at Sandra Nimmo's.

When Faith moved into a house full of lesbians in the very white South End of Halifax, it raised tensions, she tells me. Later "all the WASPs left" and Faith would find herself living with only French-Canadian and Jewish women. Faith's partner at the time was a working-class French-Canadian woman who had lost custody of her children to her ex-husband. "Her husband said if she took him to court he would say she was a lesbian so she would have no visitation rights," Faith recalls.

"I think that there were maybe lots of Black lesbians who lived in the fifty or so Black surrounding communities," Faith speculates. She recalls a pair of Black sisters who were lesbians, but who didn't come to the predominantly white women's events.

She was denied housing, but it was hard for Faith to determine if she was being harassed or discriminated against because she was Black, lesbian, or both. Not a feminine woman, Faith couldn't "pass" as straight even if she wanted to. If they used the N-word or called you a dyke, then you'd have an inkling, she tells me. "Or they could use a combo and you're not sure which one they meant more."

One hundred percent out, Faith was also told "not to be going into the community if I was a lesbian—the Black community—because it was sinful." Still, the theatre student was involved in the Black Students' Union at Dalhousie University (there was "a lot of homophobia," she says), worked as a tutor in Beechville, and volunteered at the North Branch Library.

Being "booted out of the black community for being queer" prompted Faith to move back to Toronto. "Enough of this shit," she remembers thinking. She is now a well-known musician, labour activist, and advocate for people in prison, and much of Faith's art has centred on the legacy of Africville, the African-Nova Scotian settlement on the shore of the Bedford Basin destroyed by the city in the 1960s, where her family had lived for five generations.

▼

APPLE's goal, says Susan, was political activism. "We really wanted to move and change things. This was the seventies," she says. "We had a telephone tree to let people know about all the things that were going on."

Susan remembers two women, regulars at The Turret, one of whom was a sex worker, coming to one or two APPLE meetings to pitch the idea of starting a women's bar. There weren't "enough of us," Susan says.

Nancy, who had moved to her place in the country by the time the group was formed, remembers hosting some APPLE women at her home. They spent their days clearing the land and their nights singing and laughing, sleeping in sleeping bags scattered around her old farmhouse. It was a "great group," Nancy says.

The group ran on consensus, and encouraged members to air any grievances before getting on to official APPLE business. Though Sandra Nimmo enjoyed listening to what the different APPLE women had to say, she admits that she is a person "who likes to do something and put a lot of energy in and get something done"—so she found meetings frustrating.

"In time, a newer group of lesbians became involved in APPLE and were concerned because we did not 'do' enough," Anne wrote in *Groups Dynamic*. Diane Guilbault told me in an email: "The group really was not politically active, even though individuals in the group were."

"It was a nice idea; a group that never really got going," says Deborah Trask.

Deborah remembers a meeting of approximately thirty women at Halifax's Hope Cottage to determine APPLE's final fate. A handwritten note in Anne's archives, presumably announcing that meeting on January 13, 1979, reads: "Sisters, APPLE has reached the point where we must all come together to decide her future. Many women have left APPLE, and many do not wish to be involved. Why?" The note, signed by Diane Guilbault, continued: "What are your needs within APPLE? What direction should APPLE be taking? Is APPLE a 'political' organization?"

"The heated arguments and irreconcilable difference ultimately baked APPLE into oblivion," Anne wrote.

"Over the years, young women have searched me out to interview me about the early days of lesbian organizing in the province," Deborah said at a 2SLGB history panel organized in 2018 by Pride Nova Scotia, the body representing 2SLGBTQIA+ government employees. "They want me to tell them how women all worked together towards a common clearly understood goal of lesbian liberation, and I know what I have to say is always a great disappointment to them."

"Each one of those things is a step forward," Nancy says. "Even if APPLE didn't last ten years or twenty years, it was a step forward that helped some of us come out and find out who we were."

Chapter 5

THE TURRET: A SPACE OF THEIR OWN

(1976–1982)

"Woohoo! Now you're talking!" exclaims Lorne Izzard. We're sitting side-by-side in Lorne's den, which houses his collection of disco 33s (every disco record from back then, he thinks).

"Oh my god, what a building, what a time."

Lorne's enthusiasm is emblematic of the vast majority of responses I get when I ask about the Turret, Halifax's first gay and lesbian bar-cum-community centre, run by the GAE.

"It was a time of just absolute freedom," Lorne continues. "We had our own club that was rivalling anything else in town."

"The Turret was famous across the country," recalls Walter Borden. It was "iconic."

The Turret began as a one-night disco on the third floor of the former Church of England Institute—a castle-like brick building (later known as the Khyber Building) at 1588 Barrington Street.

The idea for a GAE-run discotheque was born in 1975, shortly after Robin Metcalfe and John Lewis were banned from a bar/restaurant known as The Heidelberg for dancing with a member of the same sex.

The former Church of England Institute (later known as the Khyber Building) on Barrington Street. The Turret club was situated on the third floor.

(ROBIN METCALFE COLLECTION)

"In the daytime it was totally straight, and at nighttime it was still a straight bar, but it was a gay hangout for meeting men," says former GAE member and drag queen Randy Kennedy of The Heidelberg. "But you had to be very discreet."

When The Heidelberg's owner refused to engage in a conversation with GAE about the incident, members of the activist group decided to take their business elsewhere. They set up a meeting with the Youth Employment Society (YES)—which Robin describes as "guys with beards and long hair who were into folk music"—who were leasing the soon-to-be Turret space, which had formerly housed Sanpaka Restaurant. YES was struggling to draw people to their folk, blues, and jazz nights, and were happy to rent the space to the gay group.

The space came with hardwood floors, wainscotting, gothic peaked windows, and a turret (a spire-topped tower) that protruded over Barrington Street, for which the club was named. Sanpaka's owners had left the fabric-covered dome lampshades, which hung down from the twelve-foot ceilings, some rickety wooden tables and chairs, and a shelving unit filled with dishware adorned with dainty pink apple blossoms, which The Turret would use for ashtrays. (When the club moved five years later, Anthony Trask says, everyone took a few of the dishes home as a souvenir.)

Nearly everyone I spoke to for this book could still describe The Turret's layout in incredible detail—the winding staircase that led to the third floor, the Plexiglas Turret logo just past the second-floor landing, the smaller staircase leading up to the second level and bar, the DJ booth nestled in the bar's namesake turret, even the "dings in the walls from people hurling ashtrays." On the second floor was a youth health clinic, staffed by Dr. Bob Frederickson, who was known as Dr. Bob. Before HIV/AIDS, the main sexually transmitted infections were gonorrhea, syphilis, and chlamydia from the sailors, says Anthony. A gay doctor, Dr. Bob was also one of the founding members of the first HIV/AIDS organization in Halifax, the Gay Health Association.

The first GAE disco in the space was held in January 1976. Members of the group pooled around twenty dollars each to buy beer, which they had to haul out onto the snowy roof to keep cold because there was no refrigerator. Volunteers took turns staffing the door and the bar, and fetching the beer from outside.

All these years later, Robin recalls the thrill of that first night.

"I remember this enormous feeling of excitement that this was working—people came. People came in large numbers," he says. "It clicked from the very beginning and it was quite a joyful thing."

In that year's annual Secretary's Report, Robin described the discotheque—initially named "The Other Side"—as being "as an immediate success, drawing large crowds and creating a friendly, loose atmosphere."

Anthony Trask was all nerves during his first time at "the club," as most regulars called it. He had never been to a gay club before. That night he was supposed to attend a concert by American country musician George Hamilton IV, but the concert was cancelled. His first memory of the club—where he would soon become a volunteer—was of the shimmering chords of ABBA's "Dancing Queen."

"Anytime I hear any disco music I just close my eyes and I'm back there," Anthony tells me. At the time, Donna Summer was "huge" (before she reportedly told audience members at a 1983 concert that "AIDS is the result of your sins"—something she later denied), and Anthony would volunteer to clean up the next day, just so he could go in, lock the door and play Summer's "Four Seasons of Love" on repeat. One day another GAE member and his boyfriend walked in on Anthony while he was singing enthusiastically into his "microphone"—the broomstick.

In fall 1976 Anthony had just dropped out of Acadia and was living with his older sister, Deborah Trask, in her one-bedroom apartment. When Deborah came out to him, Anthony promptly brought her to the club.

"And the rest is history," he says.

That first night is etched in Deborah's memory.

"There was this wild character with whom I became very good friends," Deborah says. She remembers Keith Dobson—a hairdresser whom she only ever called Kitty—dancing "wildly," flipping his hair around.

"You would come home with your clothes smelling of perfume and smoke and poppers," says lesbian feminist activist Susan Holmes. "You'd have a shower and air your stuff out on the clothesline."

"It would be hard for you to understand," says Deborah. "A feeling of coming home, even though it was once every two weeks." Susan also uses the word "home" to describe the space, which she describes as warm and friendly.

The disco went from being every second Saturday night to every Friday from 9:30 P.M. to 3:00 A.M. and, according to an early pamphlet entitled "Welcome to The Turret," offered "a friendly, non oppressive meeting place for gay people in Halifax."

Soon, Deborah was attending GAE meetings.

"It didn't take me long to realize that they needed to be a bit more organized," Deborah says. "My brother tells me I'm a little bossy," she adds.

One of GAE's main goals at the time was to establish "a place we can call our own," according to the "Welcome to The Turret" pamphlet. "A place where we can meet, talk, drink, and dance together. A place to make friends. A place to be ourselves. A place run by and for the gay community," which the GAE estimated consisted of five to ten thousand in the Halifax/Dartmouth area.

"We have an opportunity to create such a space," the pamphlet continues. GAE hoped to sign a lease and open a licenced club during the week—"A time when there are no public meeting places for gay people in Halifax." The club would be a place for gay people "young and old, women and men," and would feature disco music, live performances, folk nights, and films; it could also be a quiet spot to sit and talk.

Twenty-five percent of the profits were to go to the GAE—to support political advocacy, the newsletter, and the Gayline—and the remaining 75 percent would go towards yet a bigger dream, a gay community centre.

The centre would be a place that, as the pamphlet says, would "let all Nova Scotians know that we, the gay people of Nova Scotia, are taking our rightful place in the community, open and proud of our special identity."

In 1977 membership was five dollars, which got you a laminated membership card featuring the building's turret peeking out of the clouds, illustrated by visual artist and NSCAD alumnus Rand Gaynor. Many still have that card.

Deborah was one of three GAE members who eventually did sign the lease for The Turret's space, approximately 2,600 square feet for $12,000 a year, on September 2, 1977. She still has the original document at her home.

"When it came down to it, nobody wanted to sign the lease," says Deborah. "I had a good government job where it would be difficult to get fired, so I signed the lease."

The Turret had one major advantage over David's across the street: a steady liquor license. The liquor board hearing happened only shortly after Robin, Jim, Deborah, and Anne were barred from the Jury Room.

WELCOME TO THE TURRET

The Turret is a licensed discotheque open every Friday from 9:30 pm to 3:00 am, offering a friendly, non-oppressive meeting place for gay people in Halifax.

Who are we ?

We are the women and men of the Gay Alliance for Equality and of the Nova Scotian gay community. We recognize the need of gay people in Nova Scotia for a place we can call our own: a place where we can meet, talk, drink and dance together. A place to make friends. A place to be ourselves. A place run by and for the gay community.

Why the Turret ?

We have an opportunity to create such a place. With your support, we hope to obtain a lease and to open the Turret as a licensed club during the week, a time when there are no public meeting places for gay people in Halifax. We would try to offer a place for all gay people – young and old, women and men – with the kinds of entertainment gay people want – disco music, live performers, films, folk music or just a quiet place to sit and talk.

We have another dream as well. That is someday (and someday soon) to open a Gay Community Centre. The Gay Community Centre would be a place to serve all the special needs of the gay community. A place for meetings. An office for the Gay Alliance for Equality. A place where people can come when they need help and support. A place that would let all Nova Scotians know that we, the gay people of Nova Scotia, are taking our rightful place in the community, open and proud of our special identity.

Before we can do any of these things we need your support and we need money. The Turret is run entirely by volunteer help. All the money collected here tonight, after we pay our operating costs, returns to the gay community. 25% of our profits go to the Gay Alliance for Equality, to support our political work to achieve equal rights, to publish our newsletter, the VOICE, and to operate our telephone counselling service, the GAYLINE. The other 75% goes into the Gay Community Centre Fund, towards the day when we can create a place for all gay Nova Scotians to call their own.

How can you help ?

Come to the Turret. Enjoy yourself. Tell your friends. Let us know what you like, and what you don't like. This is your place. Tell us what you want the Turret to be. Volunteer half an evening to help out (volunteers get in free). Bring in your own records, tell us what you want to hear. The Turret will be whatever we make it, together.

For more information, talk to any member or contact the Gay Alliance for Equality, P. O. Box 161, Arndale Station, Halifax B3L 4G9, or call the GAYLINE at 429-6969, Thursday, Friday or Saturday from 7 pm to 10 pm.

We can do it together.

An undated GAE flyer advertising the Turret. **(ANNE FULTON COLLECTION)**

"After that incident the bars went to the liquor board and said, "Give them their own license; we don't want them in our place," says Anthony. Deborah remembers the group's lawyer using the Jury Room incident to convince the board to grant the GAE a licence. She was appalled, but it worked.

"I was loyal to Dave for a while over at the other club," Mary Ann Mancini told journalist Allie Jaynes. "But I wanted to be where there were more people eventually." Soon, Mary Ann was also volunteering at The Turret, helping to carry booze up those three flights. "[You] felt like you almost had to do it because you wanted it to be a success; you didn't want it to disappear," she said.

For Jim MacSwain, yes, The Turret was a place to "sling beer" and make money—but primarily, it was a safe place: "People can come there and they can dance to their heart's content, they can cruise to their heart's content, they can love whoever they want to their heart's content. What can be more exciting than that?"

"You knew that the moment you stepped into the doors you were stepping into your world," says Turret regular Walter Borden. "You could just be. You could just be."

From 1979 to 1981 Anthony Trask, then GAE's resource coordinator, spent his days just around the corner in the Alliance's office on Blowers Street. Most days after work, Anthony would go home, eat supper, head right out back the door, and walk down to The Turret.

One such night, Anthony was at home primping for The Turret's Halloween soiree, letting his nail polish dry, when the doorbell rang. Long before glitter became near-synonymous with queer culture, Anthony remembers applying hobby shop "sparkles" to his face and throughout his full beard before heading to the club. "And people didn't wear sparkles," he points out. (One night at The Turret, Anthony's glitter got him noticed by a group of male figure skaters, in town with the Ice Capades, who just had to know—where did he get those sparkles?)

Already coated in glitter and sporting a shimmery shirt via Frenchys, Anthony opened the door, only to find a pair of Mormons standing outside.

"Come in!" he exclaimed. "I've been waiting to talk to you for years!"

He had been working the Gayline, and wanted desperately to know what the Mormons' stance was on homosexuality, should it come up during a call.

Those particular Mormons didn't have any answers. They did, however, return on a separate occasion. "They had searched out my request for them and all they could find is that it would be considered premarital sex. So, under that it was not allowed." They left Anthony with a Book of Mormon, which he has to this day.

▼

Reg Giles lived in the Green Lantern building across the street from The Turret. The florist who had lived there before Reg had hand-painted ribbons, with fake-flower flourishes in the place of bows, above the apartment's wood panelling. Reg painted over the "tacky" decor, but it didn't much matter; after his first foray to The Turret around 1979 he spent most of his time across the street anyway.

Reg spent so much time at the club—first as security and later as maintenance, coat check, and bar staff— that he often slept in the old brick building. Anthony remembers arriving at The Turret to the sound of Reg playing the piano.

The pride Reg took in the space is palpable forty years later.

"I kept the floors sparkling," he says, adding that when he was last in the building for The Turret Resurrection Disco event in 2013, those same floors "were a mess."

"After I stripped and refinished the floors people tapped their toes on the floors to make sure they weren't wet." And they may well have been; Katherine MacNeil admits that her "sin" was sprinkling extra wax on the floors to make them more slippery—"so you could dance better!"

And then there was the music—the "best this side of New York," says Reg—spun by Chris Shepherd. The two had been buds during their Dartmouth High School days, but became close while they were both working at The Turret.

On the weekends, Chris, who also bounced and DJed at The Piccadilly Club, played everything from disco to bluegrass. "They could put 'I's the B'y' on and I'd be jumping," says Faith Nolan, who loved "shaking it" at The Turret. Still, for Faith—who had come out into the lesbian and queer bars of Toronto (The Blue Jay, Howard Park, and Momma Cooper's)—having *only* The Turret "felt like it was twenty-five years behind."

It was the heyday of Gloria Gaynor, says Susan. "'I Will Survive' was on every Saturday night at least once; I could dance to it all night long."

According to the 1978 Turret Social Membership Survey—completed by 25 percent of The Turret's membership—men dusted off their dancing shoes more regularly, with the median attendance being six nights a month, versus four nights for women. Women were slightly heavier drinkers (four drinks to the men's three-and-a-half) and smokers (65 percent to the men's 57 percent).

Men preferred disco above all else, while women respondents were largely indifferent (though it is noted in GAE minutes that Anne Fulton requested more waltzes). Shepherd himself was partial to the glitz and glam of disco, his favourite songs being "The Boss" by Diana Ross, "I Will Survive," and "Heaven Must Have Sent You" by Bonnie Pointer.

Men were mostly united in their wish for a "more elaborate lighting system" for the disco (61 percent)—slick light shows complete with lasers were very "du jour" in gay clubs across North America—while nearly the same number of women were happy with the current lighting.

Unsurprisingly, the atmosphere was considered the most positive feature, followed by the fact that it was "gay and one can be oneself there," (according to 26 percent of women and 41 percent of men).

On weekends people often lined up waiting to get in, with the lineup winding down the main staircase. The space would fill up around 11:00 P.M., says Katherine, and it would be "hopping."

"When that dance floor was full, the building used to move," she says.

Being shoulder-to-shoulder with fellow community members made the space feel "homey," says Reg.

"Your weekend did not exist without it. It just didn't," Walter says of The Turret. He says Friday through Sunday it was the same feeling. "It was just this great relief." Every Saturday before going to The Turret, Walter would gather with friends to watch *Monty Python*, he adds.

After he moved The Alternate Book Shop from across the street, Tom Burns spent Thursday through Saturday on the second floor of The Turret's building. At 2:00 A.M. he would close the shop and head upstairs for a dance or three. On Saturdays, The Turret would be open until 3:00 A.M. Then they were off to the Garden View Restaurant on Spring Garden Road, says Walter.

The Turret was the epicentre of gay life and activity in 1970s Halifax. "It became the hot spot to go," says Chris.

"It happened at the right moment," explains Robin. It was 1976 and "the number of people coming out and exploring their sexuality was increasing rapidly because of gay liberation, and the place filled a void." It had been nearly a decade since the "summer of love" and it would be years until anyone in Halifax would hear of HIV/AIDS.

"If I could time warp, drop me off in the '70s and don't bother coming back to pick me up," Chris jests. "It was such a fun time, once you got to club age. You got dressed up; you wanted to feel good; you wanted to look good." There were still bills to pay, but Chris calls the 1970s a "freewheeling" time.

"We had a lot of fun; we had a lot of sex," says Reg. "It was the sexual revolution," after all.

The Turret's two levels made the space ideal for cruising; atop the stairs you could scan the dance floor for someone with whom you might want to share a dance (or more). It was also the perfect set-up for a drag or variety show. Reg rebuilt the stairs to the bar so they were wide and built a thrust stage to better accommodate performances.

"They were events. We rehearsed for months," says Reg, who organized and hosted many shows. "It wasn't just a show; it was *the* show." The shows were "more glamorous" back then, he says.

The Sunday of the first variety show, a gaggle of Turret members volunteered to cook a buffet meal of roast beef, salad, and dessert, Reg wrote in his personal account of the time, "Peanut Butter And Jam Sandwich (Thru My Eyes)" on the GayHalifax wiki. Reg made red curtains; stage lights from apple juice tins, coloured gels, and household dimmer switches; and "handheld spotlights made from stovepipes and a 75-watt floodlight." The backdrop, made from silver thermal heat blankets, twinkling Christmas lights, silver garland, and silver stars, completed the look.

Shows-to-come would feature a bevy of local queens and musicians, including Halifax's original drag mother, Sugar (Tommy Miller), Peenee and

GAE founding member Tommy Miller in drag as Sugar at The Turret. **(JIM DEYOUNG COLLECTION)**

Reg Giles during a show at The Turret. **(JIM DEYOUNG COLLECTION)**

Jerri, Lily Champagne (Randy Kennedy), and Joanne Bond, who belted Janis Joplin's "Mercedes Benz" among other blues and rock tunes. Reg remembers one of the queens singing a Melba Moore song live, hitting a high C. The shows' gloriously gay themes included "Those Gay Old Days," "God Save the Queens," and "Christmas in July (Don We Now Our Gay Apparel)," the latter teasing that "Santa may even make an appearance and surely some of his elves and fairies will be there."

In May 1979, on the heels of the February 14 acquittal of the officers of Pink Triangle Press (which published the *Body Politic*) on obscenity charges, the GAE held a benefit cabaret to assist with the costs of fighting the Ontario government's forthcoming appeal of the verdict. A year later the GAE marked the first anniversary of the acquittal with a show they called the Pink Triangle Day Affair. The show included Jim MacSwain and Clairemarie Haley as Gertrude Stein and Alice B. Toklas, drag queen Ezzie performed *Rocky Horror Picture Show*'s "Sweet Transvestite," and Reg Giles performed a trio of songs including "Mack the Knife."

In 1981 Reg, Tommy Miller, Randy Kennedy, Emerald Gibson, and Dean Roach were part of a group of performers who founded the Gay Artists Musicians and Entertainers Society (GAMES), which went on to have fifty-two members who put on shows at The Turret and, later, at Rumours.

▼

Randy Kennedy was seventeen when he first started going to The Turret. That first night, he found himself sitting at the bottom of the stairs, wondering if he should just go back to The Heidelberg. His age wasn't the issue; he simply wasn't a member.

Along came Sharon Gesner, a Turret regular who "dressed femme but was butch as hell," says Randy. "And she said 'Honey, what are you doing down here?' I said, 'Well, I'm not a member' and she said, 'Come with me. I'll sign you in, but if you start any trouble I'm going to beat your ass.'"

Ready for his big debut, Randy was wearing black satin pants, a black satin shirt, a gold sequinned belt, and a matching gold sequinned tie. Reg greeted Randy at the door, looked the new kid up and down and said, "We could hang you up like a mirror ball," says Randy.

A poster for a Gay Artists Musicians and Entertainers Society (GAMES) show. **(JIM DEYOUNG COLLECTION)**

Once inside, Randy laid his eyes on a couple, two men, dancing together, spinning and dipping. "And I had this feeling of, 'I'm home,'" he tells me as we sit in his apartment in Montreal in spring 2019. It is easily the most glamorous studio apartment I have ever seen: everything is gilded gold and adorned with jewels; there are several mini chandeliers, left by another tenant in the parking garage. There are several bedazzled drag headpieces, one with both a pink triangle and a rainbow motif, and Randy's workstation is topped with dozens of handmade drag earrings. (A femme with an affection for all things glitter and gems, I am in heaven.)

Flanking his bed are two painted self-portraits, one of Ms. Lily Champagne and one of Randy, out of drag, wearing a smart leather cap.

At the time of our interview Randy had been performing as a drag queen for thirty-nine years. The first drag queen he ever saw perform was his soon-to-be drag mother, Sugar. Sitting on the floor of the Turret, in the front row, Randy was in complete awe. Sugar descended the stairs sporting a two-piece silver satin pantsuit and a silver cape, lip-synching the words to "Big Spender."

At the bottom of the stairs Sugar squatted down in front of Randy and popped her boobs right out, Randy tells me, making a "pop" sound with his mouth. "Everybody was laughing and I didn't know what to do," he says. Sugar simply tucked her breasts back into her suit and planted a big ol' red-lipsticked kiss on Randy's forehead.

A week later, Randy approached Sugar, a.k.a. Tommy Miller, at the club and complimented him on the show. "Who are you, cunt?" Tommy responded. Before Randy could walk away, Tommy had charmed him. "Oh, I was just joking with you," he cooed. They were instant friends.

The first time Randy tried drag was the Halloween after that fateful show.

He was still living with his parents and hadn't told them that he was gay. When Randy told his mother that he was dressing as a woman for Halloween, she thought, "Oh, this is going to be funny!" When Randy emerged from his bedroom wearing a hand-sewn cream-coloured satin gown with a fur stole, a matching hat and veil, rhinestones, and with his hair "did," his father exclaimed "Jeeeeeesus Christ."

"You look nice," was all his mother said. At The Turret, Randy met up with Sharon and her ex-girlfriend-cum-best-friend Hazel. Sharon wore a feather mask and a matching skullcap and jumpsuit, while Hazel was dressed up as Elvis Presley: white suit, gold belt, sideburns and all.

Later, when Randy moved out of his parents' house in Dartmouth, he would move in with Tommy in Halifax. Randy slept on the couch of the Church Street rooming house that was home to Tommy and two other gay men. When he started working at The Turret as a busboy and bartender, Randy moved out and into the Morris Street apartments. The former mansion was "just so gay" says Randy; there was even a grand Scarlett O'Hara–style staircase.

Like the Green Lantern building, the Morris Street apartments were home to a host of gay men. Chris Shepherd, who lived across the hall from Jim DeYoung, says that "gay kids told each other about the apartments when they left."

"My apartment, in particular, on the ground floor was like a revolving door," Chris says. "There were people stopping by for coffee and a chat all day long. Same upstairs. Almost like a community centre, without the functions of a community centre."

Chris recalls one particularly "rockin'" party in those apartments. It was Good Friday in 1981 and The Turret was closed. "We'll be the club," the men thought. Chris estimates that four hundred people came through their door that weekend.

Jim's apartment was the bar, Randy remembers, and Chris's was the dance floor. The two apartments upstairs, Randy's included, were "relax areas."

Like any good diva, Randy incorporated a costume change into the night, reappearing as his comedy character Laverne. "Hello everybody! Laverne's here!" he bellowed before launching himself down the banister. He collided with the big knob at the bottom, then flipped over backwards and landed on the floor. "And that was my entrance into that party," he says. "But everybody loved it. It was just such a good time."

"I think that was the last time that Halifax saw a gay house party like that," says Chris.

▼

The Turret staff was "like a family," says Randy. During the city's police strike Randy and a handful of staff, including Reg, slept in the club, in case somebody tried to break in.

It was Tommy who gifted Randy with the outfit for his first drag performance. Randy paired the blue satin dress with a blonde bob and blue eyeshadow. "It was hideous," he says with a laugh. Current-day Randy is mortified that he didn't shave his armpits or chest for the number. Shorn or not, he still got a rousing round of applause.

"Drag queens were a lot closer. There wasn't the bitching [at each other] that you see now." (Randy says he only got through one episode of *RuPaul's Drag Race* before throwing up his hands and saying, "That's enough.")

Randy eventually settled on the name Lily Champagne, a take on the song "Lili Marleen," made famous by his favourite singer, the gender-bending Marlene Dietrich. In 1981, Lily brought home the Miss Gay Halifax crown.

In the early 1980s Randy spoke at two Civil Rights Committee–sponsored events on the politics of drag; the first was entitled "Drag: Sex Role Satire or Sexist Putdown" at The Turret in December 1980.

The write-up in that month's GAE newsletter read: "The value of drag has been questioned hotly, particularly by lesbian-feminists, and on a national level by the well known film, 'Outrageous' starring Craig Russell." It noted that both "men and womyn" were invited to attend what "promises to be a very lively discussion."

"The first one, it was me, alone, and a whole room of that gang of women," says Randy, referring to the lesbian feminist crowd. "They're sitting there in overalls and workboots and buzz cuts...and they are asking me why I dress like a woman."

Before the event ended, Randy said to the crowd, "Listen, you're coming onto me really hard here because I dress as a woman and I perform, raising money for this place. This is an open space for everybody and we have to be more accepting here."

The second discussion, in November 1981 with Lulu Keating, went much better, Randy tells me, though GAE executive minutes described the event as having "a large if occasionally acrimonious crowd of both men and women."

▼

On Wednesdays Faith Nolan and Dale Cavanagh played folk music (billed in one newsletter as "Illustrated Fingerings") and on Sundays gay Christian group Sparrow used the space for their weekly meetings (which often ended with a couple of hours of dancing, according to Chris, who DJed).

Even before Wormwood's Dog and Monkey Cinema made the former Turret space its first permanent home in 1983, the "Turret Cinema" presented titles including Barbra Streisand's *Funny Girl*; a John Waters/Divine double bill of *Pink Flamingos* and *Female Trouble*; *Janis*, about Janis Joplin; and David Bowie's sci-fi cult flick *The Man Who Fell to Earth*.

During the 1981 provincial election the GAE invited the candidates from all three provincial parties to attend the Pink Triangle Affair to celebrate the acquittal of The Body Politic and the first ever Pink Triangle Day at The Turret. Only Alexa McDonough, the recently elected leader of Nova Scotia's New Democratic Party, accepted. That night, Deborah Trask, who had been living in McDonough's basement, met Alexa at the building's front door. Alexa was nervous. "It was a major social event" and there was a lineup to get in, says Deborah. From the very butch to the drag queens, they were all there.

"Everyone was so astounded that she came that they were reaching out to touch her, to thank her, and I really felt that her presence validated our community," she says. It was also an eye-opener for Alexa, says Deborah.

"Mrs. McDonough deserves a special tribute for her understanding and courage: at least you did not appear to be threatened by our sexual preferences as the other candidates apparently were," read an article about the affair in the March 1980 edition of the Dalhousie University gay group's newsletter, the *Glad Rag*.

▼

The Turret's clientele was predominantly white. Chris Shepherd had grown up on a dirt road amongst the open fields of a small African-Nova Scotian community in Dartmouth dubbed the "Crichton Avenue Extension." Chris estimates that there were a dozen Black regulars at the Turret.

"I have found that in the gay scene, nationally, from coast to coast, there is an unwelcomeness of Blacks into the bars and clubs," Chris told me in 2016. "Blacks have never been made to feel welcome at gay establishments.

"As a result, a lot of Blacks who are gay would not go out."

Walter Borden notes that Black Haligonians (including his Nova Scotia Project peers) frequented the Black-owned Arrows Club and Club Unusual. "The white kids didn't go to the Arrows Club," says Walter.

Like The Turret, those spaces were sorely needed, given that some bars "didn't want Black people," says Lorne Izzard. "They didn't want you there, but couldn't make a big fuss." Lorne remembers the management at one establishment switching the music to easy listening or country in an attempt to coax the Black clientele to leave. (This particular attempt failed miserably, as many of the Black bar-goers had grown up in rural areas, Lorne says with a chuckle.) Service would dwindle and then you would be cut off, with no explanation, he says.

But Lorne remembers when Turret drag shows began to draw crowds of older, straight Black folks from the Prestons and Uniacke Square. It all started when a few of the Black queens invited some folks to watch them perform.

"Then it got a little bigger, and a little bigger," says Lorne. "And then all of a sudden you're seeing sister so-and-so walk in from the church and you go, 'Oh lord we're in trouble.' But no, they were coming to see the show." They had seen female impersonators while away on vacation, and The Turret's three-dollar cover charge was a deal. Randy remembers a triad of Black drag queens, Peenee, Travis, and Jerry, who went by Nunya and Her Business.

Lorne Izzard with friend Joanie Billard in the late 1970s. (JIM DEYOUNG COLLECTION)

Early on in my research, I had heard of a white drag performer who dared to don blackface for a Grace Jones number in The Turret. When I asked Lorne if he knew anything about the "incident," he replied with a laugh: "Oh yeah, Honey, I was there. I shut it down." Mid-performance, Lorne marched right up to the front of the room and said, "No, no, no! This can't go on."

"I went to the managers and I said, 'You cannot allow blackface performance in front of me," he says. "I shouted them right down."

Lorne doesn't think the young queen meant "anything by it, other than performing as a Black woman." But still, he says, "Do your research."

It never happened again, says Reg.

▼

The Turret was a place that could accommodate both the camp of drag and the seriousness of the activism, says Jim MacSwain. "That was really important that those sides of the equation could come together," he says.

"There were many different sects of LGBTQ people in Halifax, and everybody was included at The Turret," Susan says. "It was the one place where it didn't really matter what was going on—you were okay."

"You wouldn't like to go anyplace else and dance with each other," says Lynn Murphy. "Where would you meet a whole bunch of lesbians that you didn't know?"

According to Lynn, when people from, say, Boston would arrive at The Turret they would be perplexed. "But there's men here," or "But there's women here," she remembers them saying.

Having both female and male regulars gave The Turret a "very different atmosphere," Anthony Trask tells me.

Turret regulars were still, however, 64 percent men. (They were also young; the median age was twenty-four for men and twenty-six for women.) Of the women who responded, equal numbers (38 percent) identified as gay and as lesbian; 6 percent identified as either bisexual or dyke; and 12 percent identified as straight. The numbers were more decisive for men, with 88 percent identifying as gay, 10 percent as bi, and only 2 percent as heterosexual.

The women and men "operated on two different orbits," says Anthony.

When The Turret opened in 1976 some women migrated from house

Anne Fulton (left), Deborah Trask (centre), and an unidentified person at The Turret.
(ROBIN METCALFE)

parties to the club, taking up a corner of the L-shaped alcove that was dubbed "Dyke Corner." It would be a year and a half—June 1977— before The Turret would hold its first official women's night.

Katherine remembers some of the different groups of women who would frequent The Turret. There was one group whose matching tweed jackets earned them the nickname "The Tweed Group." There were "the more rough-and-ready denim/workboots–type people," but the majority were outfitted in checked shirts and jeans.

"The only people who wore dresses, though, were Tommy [Miller] and his friends," Katherine says with a laugh.

Lynn and her friends had heard of butch/femme culture, but they "didn't see a lot of it at the club." "I had come in with a wave of lesbian feminists and I think the butches did not trust us," Lynn adds. (Some lesbian feminists rejected the strict gender roles enacted by butch/femme culture.)

In response to a survey question which asked if there was a "certain crowd or individual type which cause a person to feel uncomfortable" at the club, both men and women singled out "some lesbians," "fighting women," "dykes," and "truck drivers."

"Odd, somewhat, that just as many women found these 'troublemakers' a detriment [as] did the men, although the women used more polite language," noted Turret Management Committee member Bill Gordon in his survey report. Typical comments from the men, he wrote, ranged from: "certain persons who continually cause fighting problems"; "pushy diesel dykes with chips on their shoulders"; "The Turret tends to attract bulldykes who insist on being top dogs"; and "weed the lesbians out from the dykes and you will get a larger crowd, especially women."

Comments from women included: "If (these) people make trouble there amongst themselves, it's going to cause a person to stay away"; "there are four or five girls who constantly cause trouble"; "the young ladies who seem to think that it's a place to get drunk and start fights"; and "being female, proud of it and comfortable with it, I object strongly to that certain type (which attends on weekends in particular) of female who come dressed in men's clothing (suits, etc.) or dirty work-type clothing."

"The men had just as many fights as the women, as far as I'm concerned," says Reg, noting that the first person to slap him at The Turret was a man. "It was a little bit harder to control some of the women because they were strong."

The first time Sandra Nimmo went to the club, a brawl did break out. "I thought, 'Oh, I've gotta get out of here, I don't want to get mixed up in that," she recalls. On her way out, Sandra told her friend that she didn't want to get caught up in "whatever the guys are doing." When her friend told her that the fight was between two women, Sandra thought, "Oh, even worse!" she says with a hearty laugh.

"I don't think we ever had to have the police," recalls Katherine. "I think we always managed it by ourselves."

It's important to remember, Robin says, that it "was an aspect of tough, lesbian working-class culture. They were tough because they had to be tough," he says.

The same survey question exposed ire for "catty" effeminate men and "pansies"; "stereotypes left over from the '50s and '60s"; "snobs"; "straights"; and "the management."

This disdain for queens and bar dykes could be attributed to a rejection of the previous generation's expressions of gay and lesbian identity, and of widely heralded stereotypes. The answers may have also exposed not only a degree of internalized homophobia but divisions based on class.

Butch/femme roles continued to be played out into the mid-1970s, "particularly for working-class women," says Deborah, while "the university crowd was going to be more on the feminist side. There was a bit of class difference there."

In the summer of 1977 GAE member and NSCAD alumnus Rand Gaynor was solicited to paint two murals in The Turret. One was to depict gay male sexuality and the other was to portray lesbian sexuality. Rand, who also designed The Turret's logo, was known for his airbrushed (often homoerotic) nudes, Robin Metcalfe wrote in his essay for the 1997 edition of *Queer Looking Queer Acting.*

Rand began work on the first mural—his nod to lesbian sexuality—while much of the GAE Executive was away at the national gay and lesbian conference in Saskatoon. "Upon our return we were presented with a beautifully executed mural on the back wall of the Turret that we were told might appeal to the women," Anne wrote in an earlier draft of her *Groups Dynamic* article. The group "stared aghast" at the freshly painted mural—later dubbed "tits and lipstick"— which featured two thin torsos with perky breasts, bolts of electricity coursing between their nipples. A ribbon of lipstick swirled around the figures and a tube of silver lipstick floated at the bottom right corner of the painting. "Although many women protested, there were men who liked the mural, and some women too," Anne continued. Then-chairperson Anne voiced the concerns of many women but "wasn't particularly effective," she wrote. She "grumbled" about her lack of success at a subsequent APPLE meeting.

"The APPLES decided to take matters into their own hands, and on that night, APPLE's most notorious action was born," Anne continued. A few nights later, several women with handbags—which were quite out of character, Anne wrote—quietly approached the back wall of The Turret. "Before anyone realized what was happening," Anne wrote, the women had spray painted "sexist"; "keep your hands of [sic] my sexuality," and "this is a crime against women" over the offending mural.

"I missed all the fun," says Deborah of the action.

"Some of the most well-attended and volatile meetings of APPLE and GAE ensued, along with lots of position papers being presented both at the meetings and at the dances themselves, both against and in support of the women and their action," Anne wrote.

At the August 3, 1977, GAE general meeting, Clyde Richardson, who sometimes chaired the GAE, suggested that the women involved should be barred from The Turret indefinitely, and that the two GAE members involved should be censured.

At that same meeting, GAE member Karen MacKay read a statement prepared by the women involved.

> *As women struggling for control of our own bodies and sexuality, we can only interpret [the painting] as an insult.... It essentially denotes women's breasts as sex symbols, which is an extension of the* Playboy *image of women as 'tits and ass,' in other words, sex objects.*
>
> *Add to that a style of painting which portrays women's bodies in a fantasy form unrelated to female physiology. To us it is not a meaningful symbol but a parody of the worst aspects of stereotypes about women and lesbians.*

Though their actions were not meant to portray disrespect for, or an unwillingness to work with, the GAE, the women felt they "had no forum in which to negotiate the painting's presence and therefore reacted to a blatant insult with a forceful response." If it had been simply painted over—as it later was—"there would have been no opportunity to publicly express the depth and nature of this insult."

In the end, Anthony Trask put forward that the GAE take no action against either the people responsible for painting or defacing the mural. The men's mural was never painted.

Today, the mural presumably sits—graffiti and all—under forty-plus years of paint. In 2013 as part of the NSCAD Queer Collective's Turret Resurrection Project, artist and then-NSCAD student Genevieve Flavelle recreated the mural—spray paint and all—on that very same wall.

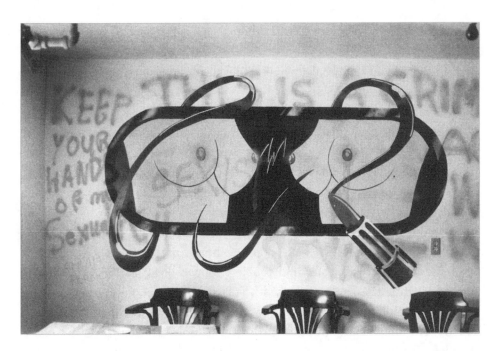

This mural, painted on a wall at The Turret by Rand Gaynor, was meant to depict lesbian sexuality. Some women, who found the depiction offensive because it "portrays women's bodies in a fantasy form unrelated to female physiology," spray-painted over the mural. **(ROBIN METCALFE)**

▼

When shit hit the fan, though, Turret patrons stuck together.

Lorne remembers a night when a handful of straight couples made it to the front of the line and into the club before they realized it was a gay establishment. Faced with men dancing with men, and women with women, the men "freaked out and tried to fight," says Lorne. "These boys found out so quick how great our community can come together," he says.

Dressed in full drag, Tommy Miller led a group of queens to confront the troublemakers. The DJ turned down the music and in a matter of minutes the 150-or-so patrons of The Turret had linked arms. It was "You gotta go!" says Lorne. "You ain't playin' here tonight."

"The assholes," as Lorne calls them, "ran off with their tails between their legs."

That night it was the drag queens, lesbians, and bar staff that answered the call, says Randy. "As soon as we came back in the door, Sharon turns around and says, 'Don't worry men, we took care of it!'" he remembers.

Perhaps not surprisingly, that night was not an isolated event. The October 5, 1979, issue of the GAE's newsletter *Have You Heard* offers a glimpse into a particularly rough weekend at The Turret. On Friday The Turret's manager was beaten and robbed while making the daily deposit; on the following night, "several people were harassing gays and threw a 'stink' bomb in the front door of the Turret Building"; a bomb threat was also called in to a local radio station. The next month someone lit a fire in the stairwell of the building, and over a hundred people "trooped down the fire escape onto the street while the fire was doused." Not an hour later, revellers were back in the club dancing to a very tongue-in-cheek "Baby I'm Burnin'" by Dolly Parton. Another Friday night, a carload of people attacked three people as they left The Turret. According to the (undated) *Have You Heard* account, the three returned to The Turret and called the police, who did not respond for forty-five minutes. An appeal over the sound system for additional security yielded forty volunteers. According to the article, when the car returned "the police were sitting across the street but refused to act, then left. The crowd remained for over a half hour but the car didn't return."

▼

"That bar generated an enormous amount of money," says Deborah. "It was very lackadaisical and then money started gushing in."

From 1977 forward The Turret was overseen by a management committee (referred to as the TMC), which consisted of four members elected from the membership (two men and two women) and The Turret's manager. The TMC was also responsible for barring members for fighting, "smoking grass," or wilfully damaging the space. As I rooted through The Turret Management Committee minutes in Robin's archives, I saw that nearly every meeting included the names of people who had been banned. One member was banned for three months, and could not return until she paid the thirty-five dollars to replace a window.

According to the membership survey, the majority of people who patronized The Turret were not active within the GAE; 68 percent of patrons did not attend GAE meetings. Five percent of men who took the survey were uneasy about "the political ties between GAE and The Turret."

"It was hard to have a political group to run a bar," says Reg. "And I said it through the years: ...the bar should be set up as a separate entity that funds the GAE and the GAE should have no say in it."

According to the minutes, this very arrangement was explored by the GAE in 1981 and it was the topic of discussion at a meeting of the members in 1982.

According to Chris Shepherd, everything at The Turret became "too political for its own good."

"Everyone went to GAE meetings to vent about The Turret," he says.

In a speech in October 1981, outgoing GAE Chairperson Ed Thibodeau told members: "As I look down the road I can see the GAE diminishing its financial dependence on The Turret.

"The Turret is not the GAE, nor does it stand or speak for the Gay Alliance," Ed continued. "The Turret has, over the years, developed into a disco club meeting the needs of a small faction of the gay community."

Three percent of the women who responded to the membership survey cited the non-profit nature of the club as a main selling feature, the same percentage who cited "women" as a main perk. (Perhaps cheekily, three percent of men named the plants and "this survey" as The Turret's most positive feature.)

▼

The closure of The Turret was nearly as sudden and as surprising as its initial success.

After six terms on the GAE Executive, Deborah Trask was GAE chairperson in 1982, the year the group was forced to close The Turret.

Deborah still has the handwritten notes for her final address to the general members' meeting in October 1982. In the notes, she writes: "I have seen the GAE go through good times and bad, but when I settled into the chair last fall, none of us could have predicted, even in our wildest nightmares, the events of this past year."

"Here is a brief synopsis," her account begins. "Within a month of the '81 Annual meeting, GAE was evicted from its office on Blowers St. After a bit of hassle, we were able to relocate on Dresden Row."

Not two months later, the GAE Executive discovered that one of their fellow Executive members "was not all he appeared to be" and was, in fact, "on the RCMP payroll." According to *The Canadian War on Queers*, the GAE was in good company: "Widespread RCMP surveillance of gay and lesbian groups in Canada did take place, and it focused especially on queer leftists who were active in these organizations."

In early May—not even a month after the GAE celebrated its own ten-year anniversary in the space—the group received notice that the lease on The Turret would not be renewed.

"From that day, the Executive never had a moment of leisure time," she wrote. In the meantime, the group was booted out of its Dresden Row office and enacted a spending freeze until they could find a new space for the club.

Though the lease for the club officially terminated on August 31, the Executive was able to negotiate an extension until September 9.

The last night at The Turret was a "mega party" according to Randy. While the revellers cleared out around 3:00 A.M., the bar staff wouldn't leave until 10:00 A.M., after they finished the open liquor, of course.

That bright and sunny morning Randy and his Turret family staggered down Barrington Street, laughing, singing, and just generally carrying on. They attracted more than a few stares. "No hiding we're gay now!"

"For me it was totally heartbreaking," says Randy of the move. "Because that's where I really came out." All of the people he met, all of the new experiences, the changes in his life—"it all happened there."

"Even when Rumours opened, that feeling wasn't there," he says. "It wasn't just the club that died, it was like a whole feeling of community that sort of died with it."

Deborah tells me that she was only ever at Reflections—a popular downtown (ostensibly gay) bar in the late 1990s and early 2000s—three times. "I hated it. It didn't have that community-centre feeling that we had."

Reg Giles misses the camaraderie sometimes. "It's something I don't think any other generation is going to have."

And no wonder. "For a time, we had in Halifax what no other place in

Canada had," Deborah says. "We had a space for the gay and lesbian community that was run by the community."

"That's why people to this day have such fond, fond, fond memories of The Turret," explains Lorne. "Because it was our baby."

In recent years I have been part of a group, Friends of the Khyber, aimed at preventing the city from selling the storied building that once housed The Turret to a private buyer. In 2018 Halifax Regional Council voted to sell the building to a society set up specifically to buy and keep the building in the community—the "1588 Barrington Building Preservation Society." In April 2019 the Society announced that it would rename the heritage gem The Turret Arts Space, in honour of its storied 2SLGBTQIA+ roots.

But for many of the people I interviewed, the name The Khyber just never stuck. That building has been and will always be The Turret.

Chapter 6

RISING FEAR, RISING UP

(1980–1984)

"*Apparently someone spread the rumor* [sic] *that there was a new club in town,*" read the GAE's October 1982 newsletter. "Opening night at Rumors [*sic*] was more popular than last year's Halloween, and the second night beat even that enviable record."

After much consternation, the GAE located a suitable space for the club formerly known as The Turret, around the corner at 1585 Granville Street. Not only did the building not initially comply with fire regulations, but the GAE had to borrow over $20,000 from its own Community Centre Fund to secure a loan to lease the building.

The name was the result of a Name the Club contest and the Granville Street Rumours would be the first location of two, the second in the old Vogue Theatre on Gottingen Street. Like its predecessor, Rumours's mandate was to "provide a social centre for the gays and lesbians of the Halifax/Dartmouth area," though some GAE members expressed concerns that the private club met "only one aspect of the needs of the local gay community."

The entrance to Rumours was unmarked, an inconspicuous black door. Regardless, on opening night a group of "thrill-seekers had to be dissuaded from gatecrashing" the festivities.

"It was a great space," says Nancy Brister, who sat on the club's management board. "We were really lucky." There was a back room that you could retreat to for some quiet, and down a set of stairs was a dance floor and bar. More people were comfortable identifying as LGBQ in the early 1980s, says Lorne Izzard, and Rumours's crowd was younger than at The Turret.

By all accounts, those dance floors were packed on the weekend. "It was just wall-to-wall people," says Diann Graham. The bar never did have a strong enough ventilation system, says Brenda Bryan, and a thick layer of cigarette smoke permeated the bar.

Katherine MacNeil only ever went to Rumours once, with Anne Fulton. "It didn't feel the same," she says. "There were a whole bunch of different people involved and it just wasn't our place anymore; we didn't feel part of it. It became, I think, a much different place."

Not even a month into its reign, Rumours ran into trouble. The bar's new manager, a straight man, was purportedly bringing illegal liquor into the bar in the middle of the night, and hadn't registered the bar with the Nova Scotia Liquor Licence Board. At their next general meeting, the Alliance's lawyer told the membership that there was "a great danger that [they] could lose Rumours (and the organization itself) if an effort was not made to work together, to try to clean up the Club's operations, and to try keeping undesirable elements from infiltrating."

As that month came to a close, the GAE received a letter from a local Black performer who went by the name Blowfly. The letter was read aloud at the next general members' meeting; it raised concerns about the October 25 Blowfly Productions show held at Rumours, which was poorly attended by the "regular crowd." Both the cast and some of the bar staff believed the low turnout was because the cast was primarily Black.

"Personally I feel that there is a great deal of prejudice in the gay community towards Blacks in light of some remarks that were overheard at the door and I quote 'check all the Black people's IDs,'" wrote Blowfly. "This caused a lot of hard feelings for those who were turned away toward the gay community and could mean that most Blacks could feel uncomfortable in the Gay Community....

"So why not realize this is 1982 and we gays are the minority, so let's stick together whether you're black or white because we are all one big family," the letter continued. "Just imagine what it's like to be Black and Gay in this world and you can see it's no picnic, believe me because I know."

The bar kicked off its second month of operation by firing the manager, and by the end of the month the GAE's chairperson, treasurer, secretary, and female member-at-large had all resigned.

At a specially called membership meeting, chairperson Cyril Tracey argued that the executive and Rumours management board had been "put on trial" for action taken by the manager of Rumours without authority." In their resignation letter, Kathleen Welsh and Nancy Logeman added, "We feel that responsibility for the club is too much of a burden for mere volunteers, especially when that responsibility could involve the financial and personal future of each member of the executive."

At that same meeting a new executive was elected, which included Robin Metcalfe as chairperson, Linda Brown as treasurer, Pat Dingle as secretary, and Lynn Murphy as female-without-portfolio.

▼

The GAE entered the opulent '80s in a state of financial crisis.

At a 1982 general meeting, the Alliance's Treasurer explained: "Our financial situation is very critical and there must be no spending until the situation is stabilized." The group's money problems could be traced back to March 1980, when GAE newsletter *Have You Heard* reported: "For the next two or three months revenues at The Turret are expected to just barely meet expenses for the organization." The GAE's communications and political activities were most impacted by the budget cuts. In January 1983 the GAE's general account had a balance of $5,460, the lowest in the organization's recent history. As of April the GAE had a debt of $40,000, not including what the group had borrowed from its own Community Centre Fund. Rumours had also lost a total of $5,000 as the result of two different robberies, one of which had been an inside job.

The first sign of financial relief came after Rumours broke even in both April and May of that year, and by October the year's operating loss had almost been eliminated. By the end of November 1984, the GAE had nearly $60,000 in its general account and $17,000 in the Community Centre Fund.

▼

In January 1983 the GAE hired Brenda Bryan to manage Rumours.

"I was kind of running out of options as to where I could work because I was politically active; I was out," says Brenda.

When she applied to the position, Brenda's housemates "were totally pissed at me."

"At the time I was living in a household that was considered lesbian separatist," Brenda says, referring to a brand of feminism that encouraged women to pursue complete autonomy from men. But they eventually came around. "They were my family; they loved me," she says. "They just couldn't understand the initial decision."

Some of the men were also wary of Brenda's new role at the club. Randy Kennedy, who differentiates between the "club lesbians" and the "political lesbians," tells me that the political lesbians had a "serious, serious problem with the drag queens."

Brenda remembers being approached by a group of concerned drag queens asking her, "What are we going to do about our shows?"

"I think we need to make them bigger and better," she replied. She still marvels at the amount of time the performers put into preparing for the shows: rehearsing, sewing their outfits. Rumours even had an on-staff designer. Four times a year, the club would attract people from Montreal, New York, and beyond for the big show. In 1983 the bar hired a pianist to play Thursday, Friday, and Saturday evenings, and in 1984 Rumours was the site of an exhibit of artwork by Randy Kennedy.

Brenda, who managed the bar for three years, introduced separate nights for women and men; women's nights were on Tuesdays and men's nights were on Wednesdays, so "both sides could actually have their needs met."

"Oh my God, I so miss that," says Andrea Currie of women's nights at Rumours. "To go on a Tuesday by myself and know everybody there and just... be with my friends and my community, and dance our asses off once a week. That was really precious." Those nights, Rumours was full of life, she says.

Andrea—who grew up in Winnipeg—had yet to graduate from high school when she bought a ticket under a fake name and boarded a train for Nova Scotia. One of three adopted children, Andrea left Winnipeg without her adoptive parents' "knowledge or permission" after they returned her fifteen-year-old brother to children's aid. Her brother, like Andrea, was a Métis child who had been adopted by a settler family during the Sixties Scoop; he had been her only ally in an abusive home.

Having grown up Catholic, Andrea started a degree in religious studies at Mount Saint Vincent University (MSVU), where an aunt had previously served as chaplain. There, Andrea was introduced to the radical leftist Student Christian Movement (SCM). She moved to Toronto for a year when she was elected national student president for the SCM. It was there, at an SCM meeting at Bathurst Street United Church, that Andrea first laid eyes on an actual lesbian couple. Andrea—who had had no exposure to queer culture growing up—remembers thinking: "those two women are together." For the first time, Andrea realized that she was "really OK with that."

At twenty-one, Andrea entered into a "wonderful, passionate" relationship with a "dazzling" woman. Colleen, who was involved in the gay-positive Metropolitan Community Church (MCC), DJed at gay dances in Toronto, topless but for a harness. "It blew my world wide open," she says of that romance.

"I was all-in as a baby dyke," says Andrea. She had lavender Converse high tops, a labrys ring, a necklace featuring two interlocked women's symbols, and a series of buttons including "Commie Dyke" (which she later gifted to her child).

"I laugh about it now," she tells me.

"Coming out for me had none of the stresses [of people who had to come out to their families]," she says. "Because I really didn't have a connection with mine."

Back in Halifax, Andrea worked at and lived above the Hope Cottage soup kitchen. "I was very interested in the lesbian community because I had this relationship," she said. It wouldn't be long before Andrea and Brenda Bryan were an item. There was a "little bit of cachet to be dating the manager [of Rumours]." It was a "sweet spot to land in as a person just coming out," she says with a laugh.

"The women's nights at Rumours is proving to be a success," an unnamed person with the initials CM wrote in the newsletter *GAE presents Illicit Politics and Subversive Sex* in July 1983. "The sentiment that I have heard from women about this evening is that the atmosphere is qualitatively different. The music is ours, there's dancing, freedom, and simply the joy of being with and meeting other women....

"To those men who criticize women for being men haters and divisive—why not challenge the existing attitudes that some gay men have towards women?" the article continued.

And the women's-only nights at Rumours did have critics. A day after a women's-only International Women's Day event in 1983, a GAE member, Bill S., wrote a passionate letter of protest.

> As a male I protest the sexist discrimination of a club sponsored by a group supposedly dedicated to the betterment of <u>Human Rights</u> and <u>equality</u> regardless of sex or sexuality. In a word your actions were <u>ILLEGAL</u>.... ~~G.A.E~~ = Girls Against Everyone!
>
> I think the organizers of this event owe the men of GAE and Rumours an apology, 1) for the setback it has caused the Gay movement; 2) for the discrimination (we all know how that hurts).

Not surprisingly, Bill S. would not have the last word on women's nights.

"As a womyn who was there, I say you have missed the point," Cheryl Payne wrote in *Illicit Politics and Subversive Sex*'s July 1983 issue. "Are you protesting the idea of wimmin coming together to celebrate a day of joy and Sisterhood? Or are you protesting the fact that for one night Rumours was not filled with an overwhelming majority of men?

"Anytime my lover and I have ever gone to Rumours we have felt that we were intruders in a men's club, not a club open to both lesbians and male homosexuals," Cheryl continued. "Come on, Bill; who should be apologizing to who?"

Sorting through the GAE's Women's Issues Committee folder at the Nova Scotia Archives, I discovered an undated and unsigned letter, circulated in advance of a special general meeting called specifically to address the tension around women's nights. It reads, in part:

> It is ironic that gay men who support a club which finds its theoretical basis in the positive aspects of "coming separate" from an oppressive heterosexist society and establishing a positive enclave for homosexual people, can

question the need for lesbians to occasionally segregate themselves from males.... In fact, the development of events for all special interest groups, gay youth, gays with children, over 30's, black gays, lesbians, can only enrich the GAE's image, as well as improve Rumours' financial position.

In 1984, women's nights continued to be held every second and fourth Tuesday evening of the month. That May, Deborah Trask, Rusty Neal, Jennifer Leith, and Judi Milne wrote a letter to the Rumours Management Board with a list of woman-oriented music they hoped the club would acquire. It's a time capsule of sorts (and it makes a fantastic playlist). Listed as "priority" were: The Parachute Club (who frequently played the Misty Moon in Halifax), Heather Bishop, Holly Near, Connie Kaldor, Ferron, Judy Mowatt, Eurythmics, Grace Jones, and Cyndi Lauper. They would also take anything by Bonnie Raitt, Fleetwood Mac, Stevie Nicks, Pat Benatar, Suzi Quatro, Martha and the Muffins, Rough Trade, The Pointer Sisters, Joan Armatrading, and Casse Culver. It also included "the classics": Meg Christian, Cris Williamson, Woody Simmons, Marianne Faithfull, BeBe K'Roche, Lavender Jane, Janis Joplin, Patti Smith, Blondie, Tina Turner, The Supremes, and Donna Summer. Brenda would travel to various women's music festivals in the United States and bring back music specifically for women's nights.

"The men hated women's music, so you couldn't very well sneak it in amongst the rest of the music at Rumours," AnitaLouise Martinez says with a laugh.

"More women started to come out of the closet, more women started to come out and play, more women started to take part in things that were happening within the community," says Brenda. "It changed the demographic of the community significantly."

On Fridays and Saturdays Brenda made the men keep their shirts on; "they hated me for that." But on Wednesdays, men's nights, you could be anything you wanted to be, she says. (The freedom for men, and some women, to dance topless would later erupt into a major conflict at the second Rumours.)

As at The Turret, both female and male sex workers frequented the club; they were (and are) part of the community. In those days there were a lot of lesbians who did sex work, says Brenda, and there were a couple of women who were acting as their pimps. The only rule was that they had to check knives at the door.

"There was a strong, dedicated group of people that kept Rumours going," says Brenda, who managed a total of twelve staff, including one Mr. Randy Kennedy. "I was responsible to the Board; they fought hard to keep it a community bar, and picking me they made a little bit of a radical choice, but I think I served them well. We made money."

▼

Unfortunately, the new location continued to attract gay-bashers looking for an easy target. AnitaLouise remembers one woman, a law student, who was badly beaten after leaving the club. Though the attack left the woman with a physical disability, she "couldn't really report it because the police were not sympathetic at all," says AnitaLouise. As a result, the woman moved to Vancouver.

Mere blocks away, gay men continued to be attacked while cruising The Triangle. In spring 1981 Emerald Gibson, then owner of The Alternate Book Shop, told *The Body Politic* that the warmer months led to an increase in verbal and physical attacks. On May 9 of that year alone two men were stabbed, beaten, and robbed in separate attacks, Emerald told the paper.

Brenda was also robbed twice during her tenure as manager.

It was a Saturday night in February, and Halifax was in the midst of a snowstorm. When she got out of the car to deposit that night's returns, a man with a mask stepped out from behind a tree, pointed a gun at her, and demanded the deposit.

"I had such an adrenaline rush I took the bag and I threw it as far away from me as I could, so he'd have to go get it, so I could escape," she remembers. Once the man had taken off with the cash, Brenda hopped in the car and shouted to her assistant, Sheila, "Follow that guy!"

When Sheila realized, mid-chase, that the man had a gun, she hit the brakes and the car slid all the way down an icy hill, Brenda recounts with a laugh.

▼

In the July 1982 issue of *Making Waves*, Lynn Murphy described the early days of that new decade as a "time of rising fear and attacks from the right."

If there is one event in gay Canadian history people know, it's likely the Toronto bathhouse raids and the subsequent fight back. On February 5, 1981, nearly two hundred police officers raided the four major bathhouses where gay men gathered in Toronto. As a result of "Operation Soap," 286 men were charged with being found-ins in a common bawdy house, while 20 were charged with being keepers of a common bawdy house. In the process, Metropolitan Toronto Police caused approximately $35,000 in damage. As with the raid on Truxx in Montreal, police subjected the arrested men to compulsory VD checks.

The next night, three thousand people protested the raids, chanting, "No more shit" and "Stop the cops," as they marched from Toronto's gay village to the headquarters of the Toronto police's 52 Division, and then on to the Ontario legislature building at Queen's Park. Eleven demonstrators were arrested.

Although the march protesting the Truxx raid in Montreal had taken place three years earlier and had involved the same number of people, the bathhouse raids protest has become the stuff of legend, in a way that the Truxx protest has not. The raids prompted a series of actions, including a twenty-five-day hunger strike by Metro Community Church minister Brent Hawkes, which he used to call on government to launch an independent inquiry into the raids. In April of that year, GLARE (Gays and Lesbians Against the Right Everywhere) held "Fight the Right," a day of lesbian and gay pride in Toronto.

In Halifax, gay men fraternized at Apollo Bath, located 1547 Barrington Street. The bathhouse (which initially held both men's and women's nights) had opened in 1972, and officially became a gay bathhouse in 1974.

Anthony Trask found out about the Toronto bathhouse raids when he went to record a segment on the GAE's scholarship at radio station C100 FM at seven o'clock in the morning after the arrests. The news had yet to reach Halifax's community.

As the group that ran The Turret and Rumours, the GAE "had a very good working relationship with the police and we had worked hard to get that," says Deborah Trask. "It wasn't easy."

On March 4 the GAE postponed its regular business to hear from the Alliance's lawyer, Michael Lynch, about "the rights that an individual has when confronted by the police." That month, the GAE would send five thousand dollars to the Right to Privacy Committee in Toronto, which had formed in 1978 in response to another bathhouse raid. According to historian Thomas Hooper, in his doctoral thesis *"Enough is Enough": The Right to Privacy Committee and Bathhouse Raids in Toronto, 1978–83*, the Right to Privacy Committee coordinated "the successful defence of 90% of the men charged [in 1981], and [raised] $224,000 to subsidize the cost of their legal fees."

Nationally, groups such as anti-abortion group Campaign Life, the anti-gay Renaissance Canada (who sponsored Anita Bryant's Canadian tour), and the Ku Klux Klan (KKK) were attempting to roll back the gains made throughout the 1960s and '70s.

Sifting through the various GAE newsletters in Deborah Trask's files, I came upon an article by Carol Millett on the Ku Klux Klan in the Spring 1981 issue of LGB publication *Making Waves*. The Klan's Toronto boss had recently revealed the KKK would set up shop in Nova Scotia. Carol started the article with a list of violence perpetrated by the KKK against lesbians and gays in the United States. The Klan was not "embarrassed to admit that we endorse and seek the execution of all homosexuals." The article continued:

> *These physical and political attacks on gays and lesbians, which are becoming more frequent and intense, are not isolated events. They are part of a growth of right-wing ideas that find expression in organizations like the Klan. Reactionary ideas are nurtured in conditions of economic and political crisis: massive unemployment, skyrocketing inflation, cutbacks in Social Services, increases in Military and defense budgets. While the masses of people are looking for some kind of solution to these problems, the "solution" provided by organizations like the KKK is to blame blacks and immigrants for high unemployment and women and gays for causing the destruction of the family and for "perverting" children.*
>
> *But no one falls for this garbage, you say. Yet Toronto cops kill black men (Albert Johnson, Buddy Evans), Quebec Provincial Police kill native men (David Cross, shot point blank in a police cruiser), the KKK kills Communists at an unarmed anti-Klan rally in Greensboro, NC, cops in Houston Texas kill Fred Paez, local gay activist, and an ex cop opens fire on two gay bars in Greenwich Village, killing two young men. 1980*

was a busy year. The Toronto and Quebec cops and The Klansman were acquitted. The freedom to murder blacks, natives, communists and gays is scary enough, but is it not more frightening to have so little public outcry or opposition to such acts of violence?

In my travels through the archives, I have not found anything else that reads as if it could have been written today. It is downright eerie.

Robin Metcalfe wrote about the first meeting of what would become the Nova Scotia Coalition Against the KKK for the Spring 1981 issue of *Making Waves*: "The organizers weren't ready. They had booked a small room in the Dalhousie education department for a meeting to talk about the Klan. Most likely they expected the usual hard-core of political activists to show up." Instead 150 people attended the meeting, forcing them to move to a larger hall. "It was a crowd of many faces: East Indian, Chinese, white, Jewish, Catholic, atheist, women and men, straight and gay," Robin wrote. The coalition had a "broader membership than anything else that was being organized at the time," Barbara James says.

On April 11 the Nova Scotia Coalition Against the KKK, of which GAE was a member, held an anti-KKK rally at the Joseph Howe School in north end Halifax. Approximately two hundred people attended.

The KKK never did set up an official chapter in Nova Scotia.

▼

In her last address to the membership as GAE chair, Deborah cautioned that "the aims of the Society must not take a back seat to the running of a bar.

"We still NEED to work for change, to educate the public, to establish a community centre, and to fight for rights guaranteed to all other Canadians," she said.

The Speakers Bureau component of the GAE was reactivated in 1981, thanks to a motion by Lynn Murphy, and within the month the Bureau was back at Dalhousie University presenting to a group of medical students. According to a report from Jim DeYoung, the professor screened two videos: *A Special Place* (a lesbian film) and *Nick and John*. Both films, Jim reported, included long and explicit scenes of "nude lovemaking." The films were followed by what was surely an exceptionally awkward Q & A. Speakers from the bureau continued to make appearances on college and university campuses around Nova Scotia, including at New Glasgow's Aberdeen School of Nursing. In 1983, at the behest of a student, GAE spoke to a criminology class at Saint Mary's University, focusing on a "historical look at gay life in Halifax, human rights legislation, legal forms of harassment and homophobia."

The Civil Rights Committee organized panels on gays and the constitution, the politics of drag, and a women-only discussion on "prostitution" featuring Sharon Gesnor and a lawyer. In spring 1982 the small-but-mighty committee made a presentation to the federal Human Rights Commission, which included the submission of the CRC's brief on the matter, as well as poetry by Robin and Jim, and a reading from a lesbian novel by Lynn.

In October 1983 six GAE delegates made a road trip to Fredericton, New Brunswick, for a conference called "Living Gay," organized for Atlantic Canadians by FLAG (Fredericton Lesbians And Gays). Sixty delegates attended the conference, and the Saturday night social ballooned to 280 people.

Workshops included "Feminism for Faggots"; "Married Gays"; "Gay Parents"; "Aging"; "Atlantic Outreach" (facilitated by GAE staffer Clairemarie Haley); and "Bridging the Gap Between Gay Men and Lesbians," led by *The Body Politic*'s Chris Bearchell, which discussed divisive issues such as S&M, youth sexuality, public sex, and porn.

"The nicest aspect of the conference, which was prevalent through the entire three days, was the comradeship between the men and the women," Clairemarie wrote in a report on the conference. "There was such a feeling of love and strength in the room, one hated to leave.

"I just wish that more Halifax delegates were present to witness that yes, men and women can really relate and actually have a good time together, and more importantly, grow together," she concluded.

▼

In the summer of 1981 approximately a hundred people bused out to Silver Sands beach in Cow Bay on Nova Scotia's Eastern Shore for the first annual "gay picnic."

Jim DeYoung's pictures from that day are glorious. Randy Kennedy, with a mane of curly strawberry blond locks, a light blue linen shirt tied at the waist, and white skin-tight booty shorts, struts towards the camera. Chris Shepherd strikes a pose (wearing, inexplicably, a homemade pig hat) in front of Speedo-clad sunbathers. Two women get cozy on a beach blanket, one sporting a pair of overalls and bikini top, the other in jeans and a T-shirt, a necklace with two interlocking women's symbols around her neck.

Randy, who attended two of these picnics, remembers setting up on the opposite end of the shore from the straight beachgoers. The men wore G-strings and Speedos, and the group stuck pink triangle flags in the sand to mark their spot. The picnickers were mostly gay men, says Randy, and they stayed out all afternoon, feasting on barbecued food. One year Randy showed up at the picnic as comedy queen Laverne, based on a character from the *Sonny and Cher* show.

"In his green polka-dot bikini brief and matching blouse tied in a knot below his cleavage; a ladies' straw beach hat and a pair of huge Elton John sunglasses and parasol; EVERY head on the beach turned as she did the twist in the sand, dancing her way across to our flagged-off section," Reg Giles writes in his personal account of gay life in the 1970s and 80s *Peanut Butter And Jam Sandwich (Thru My Eyes)* on the GayHalifax wiki.

That same summer, several carloads left Halifax for New Brunswick to attend a gay and lesbian picnic in Moncton. "Fearing a large influx of gays and lesbians," Moncton city council passed a bylaw amendment that would forbid organized groups of more than forty people from assembling in Centennial Park. Despite the bylaw, a hundred people attended.

▼

After growing up in 1950s Amherst, Nova Scotia, Jim MacSwain had his first "very covert" gay relationships while attending Mount Allison University in Sackville, New Brunswick. After subsequently spending a year in Montreal, singing in choirs and volunteering on McGill's LGB phone line, Jim moved to Halifax in 1974.

In the late 1970s Jim became involved in the burgeoning movement to create non-profit galleries run by and for artists, known as artist-run centres.

Artist and GAE activist James (Jim) MacSwain, circa 1978. **(ROBIN METCALFE)**

Jim MacSwain gazes at the eight-foot wooden phallus he constructed for the first
Art By Gay Men show in 1982. **(JIM MACSWAIN COLLECTION)**

The visual artist and filmmaker spent much of his time at "The Argyle House" in downtown Halifax, which housed the Centre For Art Tapes, the Atlantic Filmmakers Cooperative, Doomsday (animation) Studios, and the Halifax Photo Co-op.

It was Jim's experience coordinating the cultural program for the 1978 national Conference for Lesbians and Gay Men and his Argyle House connections that prompted him to co-curate the first Art By Gay Men show, with Robin Metcalfe, in 1982.

That first exhibit included paintings, drawings, cartoons, pottery, sculpture, videos, stained glass, Xeroxes, and postcards by eight artists, including Rand Gaynor. The show's *pièce de résistance* was an eight-foot wooden phallus created by Jim. He originally constructed the prop for a video in which various gay personas encounter said oversized penis. While filming on the roof of The Argyle House the police stopped the shoot and confiscated the tape.

"What a dreadful thing to happen!" Jim says in his delightful falsetto. The police told the film crew that the switchboard at the station "lit up like a Christmas tree because of all of the people who were gathered in the windows watching this process.

"Silly us, we had no idea that we would be so visible during our shoot!"

The exhibit brought over one hundred people to the Centre for Art Tapes in November and December of 1982.

The second Art By Gay Men show was held in two parts: the first at the "Living Gay" conference in Fredericton in October 1983, and the second at Red Herring Cooperative Books that December. The last Art By Gay Men show would be held in 1987.

▼

The 1980s were Darl Woods's favourite decade, she tells me with a laugh.

In 1980, two years after she had been discharged from the military, Darl opened herself up to activism. That same year she enrolled in sociology at Saint Mary's University. Her schooling and her activism were all part of making sense of what had happened to her.

"The other part was needing to be with other people doing stuff for a cause," says Darl, who is part white, part Blackfoot, and part African-Canadian.

In the military, she explains, there was the "so-called greater good...God and country kind of thing."

Darl attended GAE general meetings, signed up for committees, and worked the Gayline.

In 1983 Darl was interviewed for the CBC program *The Fifth Estate* about her experience with the military. Darl tells me that she was "really disappointed in that interview," which made it look like, "Oh, poor me! Look what the big bad military did to me."

"I didn't necessarily want to feel like a victim anymore," she says.

Darl, who hadn't come out to her Christian fundamentalist family, told them just before her appearance on national television that she had been discharged from the military for being gay. That year, her mother asked her not to come home for Christmas (although she did call back a couple of days later to apologize).

When Darl went public with her story she says she "didn't necessarily feel supported by the lesbian feminist community." One woman asked Darl what she was doing in the military in the first place.

"You know who were really supportive, actually, were the bar dykes!" Darl says. "They got it." On the other hand, when Darl worked for the GAE a few years later, it was the bar dykes were who hardest to mobilize; one even told Darl she was offended by the word "lesbian."

Darl continued to speak out about the military's gay purge, at universities, on panels, and to reporters. "Every time that I spoke out, every time that I went on national television, every time I was on the radio, any time I did anything active like that I became re-traumatized," Darl tells me.

In 1984 five more lesbian women, based in Shelburne, NS, were ejected from the Canadian Armed Forces. The purge, according to *The Canadian War on Queers* by Gary Kinsman and Patrizia Gentile, was the "largest single and most publicized lesbian purge." In February of 1985 the *Globe and Mail* ran an article on the dismissals entitled "Lesbian 'Clique' Dismissed at Top-Secret Military Base." Darl became their spokesperson, and was interviewed by Anna Maria Tremonti on CBC Radio; her picture appeared in a newspaper alongside the story about the five women. Later that year Darl made a presentation about the purge to the Special Parliamentary Committee on Equality Rights. Years later, former NDP MP Svend Robinson, the first openly gay Canadian parliamentarian, told Darl that the commission (which was made up mostly of Conservatives) had been going very badly until she gave her testimony.

For Darl the peace movement "answered a lot of questions for me personally in terms of the military." Specifically, "how the military was used as a weapon against women."

In October 1983 Carol Millett wrote about the upcoming International Day of Protest Against Nuclear War in *Illicit Politics and Subversive Sex.* "Should we have a lesbian and gay contingent at the march and rally? I say yes because the forces that control life and death for millions are also the forces which control our lives as lesbians, gays, women, people of colour."

"A lot of women in my circle moved on to the peace movement," says Darl. Some, she says, made the conscious decision to step away from the GAE, "which we found quite oppressive, because men—even gay men—are still men, and privileged, and not recognizing that, and taking credit for a lot of stuff that women were doing."

Many of the women I spoke to for this book found community, friends, and lovers by way of the peace movement. Muriel Duckworth, a founding member of the Nova Scotia chapter of the national peace organization, the Voice of Women, was in her seventies in the 1980s and acted as a mentor and a *de facto* mother-figure to some women. Darl was friends with Muriel until she died in 2009, and was part of the group that provided her palliative care. Drinking tea in her Truro flat, Darl brings me a framed picture of her and Muriel embracing at a demonstration.

Andrea Currie was one of those women who found a home in the peace movement. In 1983, Andrea was involved in organizing a women-only gathering entitled "Women Against Militarism" at the Wentworth Youth Hostel in Nova Scotia's Wentworth Valley. It was at that retreat that Andrea met her soon-to-be-partner, Brenda Bryan. Andrea and Brenda, along with six other women, founded the United Spinsters affinity group, one of four affinity groups prepared to take non-violent direct action. (There was also Youth Action Pact, which included Chris Murphy from the band Sloan, the Never Again Affinity Group, and a men's group.)

It was a "wonderfully chaotic, very rich time in my life," says Andrea.

In the fall of 1984 Andrea was one of the emcees at a benefit concert where the a capella quartet Four the Moment was performing. She ran into

Kim Bernard in the women's washroom that night. When she told Kim how much she loved their set, the singer told her that they were looking for someone who sang low to replace Jackie Barkley, who became their manager. "In my mind I was going, 'I sing kind of low,'" Andrea tells me.

A bona fide Four the Moment fan—she had been at their first official concert—Andrea thought it was "the boldest, most audacious thing for me to think that I would ever sing with these women." The worst thing that could happen is that they will say no, Andrea remembers telling herself. And so Andrea, who wrote and performed her own songs at local coffee houses, learned the song "Harriet Tubman" from the Holly Near album she owned.

The only problem was that Andrea's Four the Moment audition coincided with her affinity group's first planned direct action. The federal Department of National Defence was holding a meeting at the Hotel Nova Scotia to teach local businesses how to sell their wares to the American military.

Andrea's designated "jail support person" was Naomi Lechinsky: if Andrea was arrested, Naomi's instructions were to call Jackie and tell her that she wouldn't make the audition.

The day of the action, while one group unfurled a banner inside the meeting room, Andrea distracted the people at the hotel's front desk while the rest of the protestors sat on the floor directly outside the meeting room. Once seated, the protesters sang and ("this is what we did in those days," she tells me) tossed each other a ball of yarn, making a giant web. The police were called and the protesters were arrested, but not before one particularly angry government official emptied a pot of hot coffee on the dissidents.

At the police station, Andrea remembers having to empty out her pockets, including her lyrics. "I was like, can I just keep these? I'm practicing for an audition," she says.

Andrea and the other protestors were held at the station until eight o'clock that night; her audition had to be rescheduled.

"So that's how they met me," says Andrea. "I think that they were intrigued."

As the protestors left the station, Voice of Women activist Betty Peterson was on the steps with a carnation for each of them. Betty and Muriel Duckworth had both been part of the larger protest outside the hotel, which made its way around back while the affinity group members were loaded into police vehicles. Fourteen activists were found guilty of trespassing (Andrea represented herself in court), and sentenced to their day already served.

Andrea still remembers her Four the Moment audition vividly.

"We used to sing a version of 'People Get Ready' and there's a bass line," Andrea tells me before breaking into song. The women told Andrea to just keep singing while the other voices came in. "I'm in this audition [thinking], 'Holy shit, holy shit—I'm singing with Four the Moment. Don't mess it up!'" she recalls.

In those early years Four the Moment mostly played protests and benefits—including one to raise funds for the Pentagon Party Poopers's (the name given to those who were arrested at the Hotel Nova Scotia protest) legal costs—followed later by folk festivals, Canadian concert halls, the Saint Lucia Jazz Festival, and more recently opening up for legends Maya Angelou on two occasions in Toronto and Angela Davis at Dalhousie University in 2018.

Andrea was a member of Four the Moment for sixteen years, until the group did a series of farewell concerts throughout Nova Scotia in 2000.

For many years Andrea was considered the only white woman in the quartet. Andrea—who felt honoured to be included in the Black community—often felt like the bridge between what was, by all accounts, a very white lesbian feminist community, and women in the African-Nova Scotian community. She was also a founding member of a group of non-Indigenous activists called Nova Scotians in Solidarity with Native People.

Nearly two decades later, in search of her birth family, Andrea discovered that she wasn't white, but had been adopted into a white family during what is now referred to as The Sixties Scoop, the "mass removal of Aboriginal children from their families into the child welfare system, in most cases without the consent of their families or bands," according to Indigenous Foundations at the University of British Columbia. Andrea was in her late thirties when she discovered her Métis identity. The first people she told when she received her first letter from her birth mother were Voice of Women activists Muriel Duckworth and Betty Peterson.

Andrea, who today identifies as a two-spirit Indigiqueer, was able to reconnect with six of eight siblings (two sisters had already died) and enjoy a sixteen-year relationship with her birth mother. She calls hers the "most positive post-adoption union experience...that I think any Sixties Scoop person could have."

▼

"For most of us, deciding to have sex with other men has meant choosing to risk social disapproval, legal harassment, clap, crabs and syphilis. But not cancer, and not death. At least now until now."

This was the opening line of *The Body Politic*'s inaugural article (which ran in October of 1981) on what would first go by the name Gay-Related Immune Deficiency (GRID). That year the Centers for Disease Control (CDC) in the US had received reports of the life-threatening lung infection pneumocystis carinii pneumonia (PCP), and of Kaposi's sarcoma, a cancer that forms in the lining of blood and lymph vessels, in young, otherwise healthy, gay men. The first Canadian case of what would later be renamed acquired immune deficiency syndrome (AIDS) was reported in March 1981.

At first no one, not the medical professionals, not the gay men themselves, knew how this "gay cancer" was transmitted. "Was it poppers?" Anthony Trask remembers thinking.

Anthony left for Toronto in 1982, where he moved in with friend and former GAE graphic designer Robert (Bob) Ertel. He remembers attending a large public meeting at a school in Toronto's gay village; at the time, sixteen cases of AIDS had been reported in Canada. "We know it's going to double to thirty-two," organizers told the crowd.

"So many people died," Anthony tells me. "All of my new friends in Toronto. It was very rapid, six months to a year. I finally understood things that my mother and father had talked about—all of their friends going off to war and two or three coming back."

In Halifax Brenda Bryan, who was managing Rumours, "had a lot of information." She knew who was sleeping with whom, who was closeted, who was married.

"It was a hard time. It was a scary time," she says. "And what was more scary was the lack of information, the lack of understanding of what needed to happen, and how we needed to protect ourselves." There was speculation, there were rumours, there were conspiracies, there was propaganda. "It was all a mishmash," Brenda says.

"At Rumours, that's where Halifax suddenly became introduced to AIDS, and that was not a fun time," says Randy Kennedy.

"Back then if someone was rumoured to have AIDS, it was like, 'Stay away from them,'" Randy says. He was working at the club one night when a friend who had been diagnosed with HIV (human immunodeficiency virus—the virus that can lead to AIDS) entered. Randy greeted him with a big hug and a kiss before fetching him a drink. "People were like, 'You touched him. He's got AIDS,'" Randy mimics in a hushed tone. But it didn't bother him. The epidemic, Randy tells me, broke apart "whatever was left of the tight community" that had existed at The Turret.

"Funny enough, but no," Randy responds when I ask if HIV/AIDS had much of an impact on the cruising scene in Halifax. At Rumours "everybody was in such fear," but Camp Hill cemetery, for example, was still a popular cruising spot. HIV/AIDS changed Randy's cruising habits though; he always carried condoms, and would turn men away if they wouldn't put one on. Sex work on The Triangle did "slow down," he tells me, when a local working boy came out as HIV positive.

According to Jim MacSwain, things did change. There was "a lot of sex" in the 1970s, says Jim MacSwain. "Which all came to a glorious halt with the start of the AIDS crisis."

"They were good times until people started getting sick," says Lorne Izzard, who went on to be heavily involved in local and national AIDS activism, specifically within racialized communities. "There were good times during that time, but your focus was different."

"You watched them change right in front of your eyes," Walter says, of friends who contracted HIV in the 1980s. He would notice that he hadn't seen so-and-so at the bar lately. "[It was], 'Oh, they died,'" he says. "And this was one after the other after the other.

"Yes, horrible stories. This generation does not understand what it was like," Walter tells me, sitting in Glad Day bookstore and café in Toronto.

In the summer of 1984, Scott MacNeil got a call from fellow "club boy" and friend Graeme Ellis. The August humidity was making it difficult for Graeme to breathe, and he asked to stay with Scott, who had an air conditioner. Graeme and his partner, Bob, stayed in Scott's bedroom, while he slept on the couch for a week. When Graeme's breathing got even more laboured, Scott and Bob took him to the hospital, where he was admitted.

"I can still see him gasping for air as he reluctantly walked into the hospital," Scott wrote in *Reflections in a Mirror Ball* on the GayHalifax wiki. Forty-eight hours later, they were told that Graeme had PCP, precipitated by AIDS. The pair took twelve-hour turns at Graeme's bedside.

Graeme died sixteen days after he was diagnosed, on September 2, 1984. It rattled Scott to his core, he writes.

Graeme's death prompted Scott to call Dr. Bob Fredrickson in search of educational AIDS-related resources. Together, Scott, Dr. Bob, former Turret Manager John Hurlbert, Arthur Carter, and Darrell Martin founded Halifax's first AIDS organization, the Gay Health Association.

According to an article in the *Gaezette* newsletter, penned by someone who went by "WB," by July 1984 there had been ninety-six reported cases of AIDS in Canada and "as many are aware, the Canadian statistics include AIDS cases with in our local community. In the past few weeks, gay men and women and Halifax have been discussing ways and means of confronting this growing health problem. The result is the formation of the Gay Health Association." The first order of business, WB wrote, was getting basic information out to the community; the group had already screened two videos at Rumours at the end of October.

In 1984 Gaëtan Dugas, who lived in Halifax from 1978 to 1982, died of AIDS-related complications in a Quebec City hospital. Gaëtan, a flight attendant who dazzled the crowds in Halifax's clubs, had been labelled "Patient Zero" of the North American AIDS epidemic. That claim was later debunked when a 2016 University of Arizona study determined that the virus could not have originated in the late 1970s, and that the term "Patient 0" originated from a study in Southern California, in which Gaëtan had been labelled as "Patient O—"O" for "Out(side)-of-California." The O was mistaken for a zero and the label was immortalized in Randy Shilts's 1987 book documenting the history of the AIDS epidemic, *And the Band Played On.*

"The concept of Patient Zero dovetailed with a popular desire to displace the source of contagion as far as possible from white, heterosexual America," Robin Metcalfe wrote in his essay "Light in the Loafers: The Gaynor Photograph of Gaëtan Dugas and the Invention of Patient Zero." "Gay, Francophone, an international traveller, Dugas fit the bill."

"So many, so many" people died, including former GAE Chairperson Clyde Richardson, says Deborah Trask. This is the common refrain when I ask anyone about the onset of the AIDS epidemic. The transcripts of my interviews are punctuated with the names of loved ones who died of AIDS-related complications in the 1980s and '90s.

"That was a big hit for our whole generation, and it affected the women too," Deborah says.

Everyone came together during AIDS, says Lynn Murphy. "When that happened, we realized we knew these guys." They danced together, she says, "and now they are dying one by one by one every week. I think that just bonded us back together."

Deborah's generation was at the "crest of the first wave" of LGB activism in Halifax, she tells me. "A lot was accomplished, but we were set right back because of AIDS."

Sitting in the kitchen of Jim MacSwain's shared abode in north end Halifax—which he and his housemates bought back in the 1970s—he tells me that before AIDS the 1970s were a real gathering of confidence and energy.

He marvels at the community's—the movement's—resilience.

"Gay liberation has continued," he says. "It was strong enough to continue through the AIDS crisis and to come out the other side."

▼

Deborah Trask moved to Nova Scotia's South Shore in 1985. Nearly a decade after she first got involved, Deborah pulled back from the GAE, though she remained a member.

If you were an LGB activist in the 1970s or early '80s you were considered a "bona fide subversive," Deborah tells me. "We were kind of part of a secret organization."

One morning in 1979, two men from the Special Investigative Unit (SIU) of the Armed Forces (whose goal was to "flush out homos," as Anthony Trask puts it) arrived on her doorstep. It was Anthony who answered the door. When the men—who wouldn't tell Anthony why they were there—started asking questions about his mother, he began to panic. It turns out that the SIU had run the plates on Deborah's car, which was a gift from her mother.

It was only later that the siblings discovered that the unwelcome visit had been because Deborah's friend and tenant had been dating a woman in the military, and had brought her home the night before. "That's the sort of thing that was pretty common," says Deborah.

Lorne Izzard remembers the day his boyfriend, a member of the Forces, arrived home after work, still in his uniform, and told Lorne through tears that he had to move out. Earlier that day he had been called into a meeting with his higher-ups, who told him, "We know where you are living and we know who you are livin' with. If you ever want to move up into officer rank you'll never do it." Lorne doesn't know how the military found out his boyfriend was gay, "because he was very closeted about it." Not only did they not like that he was living with an "out gay man," says Lorne, but they also did not approve of the neighbourhood he lived in, which was primarily Black.

Many within the GAE believe that the SIU would set up across the street from The Turret to photograph people entering and leaving the club. In *The Canadian War on Queers* Robin told authors Gary Kinsman and Patrizia Gentile that Turret patrons would often wave to the SIU from the front steps.

In 1978 Robin and Anne Fulton wrote a song entitled "The SIU is Watching You Now" (sung to the tune of "Santa Claus is Coming to Town"), which they performed at the National Conference in Halifax. The lyrics to the song are included in *The Canadian War on Queers*:

"You'd better watch out,
You'd better be sly,
You'd better keep out, I'm telling you why.
The SIU is watching you now.
They're making a list,
They're checking it twice,
They're gonna find out who's naughty or nice.
The SIU is watching you now.
They know who you've been sleeping with;
They know if you're of age.
They know if you've been gay or straight,
So be straight, for goodness sake."

"It was an intimidation thing and it got to me," says Trask. "After a while it just gets to you."

▼

The year 2018 marked forty years since Darl Wood was discharged from the Canadian Armed Forces.

"When Gary Kinsman approached me to speak out one more time to share my own story with you today, I was hesitant to re-tell my experience of having been purged from the military for being lesbian.... It is like ripping open old wounds in salt air," Darl said at the 2015 press conference for the "We Demand An Apology" network. The network was formed to "demand an apology for the historical wrongs committed by the Canadian government against LGBT people," according to its website.

Darl had recently been diagnosed with cancer, and had "decided at that point that this would probably be the last time that I speak publicly or even nationally," she tells me. "But then things started moving so quickly that I kind of got caught up in it." It was through the network that Darl finally met some of the Shelburne women for whom she had advocated all those years ago.

In November 2017 Darl was present for Prime Minister Justin Trudeau's long-overdue apology for what he called the "systemic oppression, criminalization, and violence against the lesbian, gay, bisexual, transgender, queer, and two-spirit communities," specifically, civil servants and military members.

Darl was there with her "wonderfully supportive" sister, a United Church minister. "I don't cry easily," she tells me, but as the Prime Minister delivered the apology that she had worked so hard to make a reality, Darl and her sister stood and wept.

"It just seemed like such an amazing thing that I never dreamed would happen," she says. "There's a lesson there that we can bring about change. It might take forty years, but it can happen.

"It made me proud that I was part of bringing this about," she says.

What helped was not so much the apology, Darl tells me, but getting together with other survivors, or "thrivers" as she calls them. "We don't want to be purge survivors forever," she adds.

When we spoke over the 2018 Christmas break, Darl had one more form to fill out before she could receive the payout from her class action lawsuit. "I can do a lot more healing with that [money]," the retired university professor and therapist jokes.

Today Darl's niece and her niece's partner are both enlisted in the military, and both are out. The two, who are "very appreciative of what I'd gone through," she says, were able to attend the Fredericton showing of the documentary about the purge, *Fruit Machine* (directed by filmmaker Sarah Fodey of SandBay Entertainment), in which Darl took part.

It makes it all worth it when she hears stories like her niece's and her partner's, she told me.

Chapter 7

WOMEN DOIN' IT FOR THEMSELVES: LESBIAN FEMINISM IN THE 1980s

Diann Graham was a junior high school student in the late 1960s when she saw a picture of American women throwing their bras into a trashcan on the cover of Fredericton's *Daily Gleaner*. She thought, "That's really a fair interpretation of what needs to change in order to have equality." It was a pivotal moment for the budding feminist.

Diann was an undergraduate student at Acadia University when she had her first lesbian relationship. "I looked at myself the first time I become involved with a woman. I thought, this feels right!" says Diann. "This is me!"

"It's a big move for a nineteen-year-old to say, 'Church is wrong, parents are wrong, police are wrong,'" she adds.

In the late 1970s Diann attended a national lesbian conference in Ottawa with hundreds of other women. She experienced a "sense of euphoria" being with that many lesbians—*who actually said they were lesbians*—tackling issues that affected their lives.

It was there that Diann—who had been completing a master's degree in London, Ontario—met a group of women from Nova Scotia, including Anne

Fulton, Diane Guilbault, Rusty Neal, and Barbara James. There were roughly ten women from Halifax at that conference, Diane Guilbault remembers. After perusing the *Sisters Lightship*—a lesbian newsletter produced by women in Halifax—Diann thought "this is pretty together stuff." That experience prompted her to move to Halifax in 1978.

"That was a time of great lesbian and gay, I would say, awakening," Diann says of the late 1970s. In London, Diann had been involved in the London Lesbian Collective.

"I think that there were sort of the lesbian feminists who tended to work with women on issues the women's movement was working on," says Diann. "And I think there was another whole group of lesbians who saw their allies as gay men. And I think that both tracks were equally as engaged and involved in the changes that we have seen over our lifetime."

In Halifax, Diann was on the organizing committee for International Women's Day "for years, and years, and years."

In 1980 the police told the group, which had gathered at Victoria Park, that they would have to march on the sidewalks because they didn't have a permit, though they had always marched on the street. After some back-and-forth, Susan Holmes "grabbed a great big sign and went out and stood in the middle of the street and said, 'We're going to march in the street,'" Diann says with a laugh. "And away we went." (Susan doesn't remember that specific IWD, but "had that kind of energy in those days," she says.) The next year the police informed the women that they couldn't have a permit because they had been "disruptive" the year before. Organizers convinced city councillor Deborah Grant to intercede and secure a permit.

It was empowering to walk down the street and call attention to issues such as women's poverty, safety, fair pay, oppressive governments, and nuclear issues, says Naomi Lechinsky of IWD.

"So many women had joined us. It was very powerful," she says.

Originally from the prairies, Naomi was living in Charlottetown in the mid-1970s, hitchhiking to Halifax with her one gay friend on weekends. A hippie with hair nearly down to her knees, she recalls with a laugh, people thought she was quite odd. "I didn't look like a dyke," she says. The Turret was "a little more rough" than her life as a hippie in the country, she says. "I remember a woman asking me to dance and being naive. And that didn't go over very well with her girlfriend, which I didn't even know." The bar was where Naomi first met Anne Fulton.

"Lesbian feminists were just so happy to meet each other," she says. Naomi first found community through Women Against Violence Against Women (WAVAW)—formed in 1980 by Cathy Dodds and Vicki Wood to organize Reclaim the Night—and through the anti-nuclear movement via Voice of Women Nova Scotia.

In 1983 a truckload of women made the trip from Halifax to Cape Breton to see American lesbian feminist icon Kate Millet speak as part of Sydney's International Women's Day celebrations. Millet, who authored the 1970 phenomenon *Sexual Politics*, was brought by a group called Women Unlimited (a group that focused on employment for women) for their first provincial women's conference, which was billed "Women and the Economy." Home alone on New Year's, organizer Cheryl AuCoin simply looked up Millet's name in the New York phone book and called and invited her to come. It was a coup for the seaside steel town. Lynn Murphy, who attended the event along with Diane Guilbault and Darl Wood, remembers Millet telling the group of Halifax women how impressed she was with the grassroots feminist organizing taking place in such a relatively small locale.

The International Women's Day march in 1981. Diann Graham is at far left. **(DIANN GRAHAM COLLECTION)**

"We were so alive; we just believed in the possibility of possibility," says Naomi. "I don't think anything stopped us. We just did it."

▼

In the 1980s Reclaim the Night swelled to include numbers that ranged from two hundred to five hundred women and children. The march wound through streets where women had been assaulted, or areas "particularly dangerous to women." Women nailed signs to poles stating: "A woman was raped on this spot."

"It felt scary," says Diann Graham of her first Reclaim the Night. "Like the first Pride marches felt scary."

In 1981 Diann wrote her sister about the march. "It's hard to mobilize resistance after years of learned passivity, but hopefully in our hearts some small will to resist will spread." That year the organizing committee brought Rita MacNeil, a Cape Breton–born singer and feminist activist, who had sung at various rallies and events in Toronto, to Halifax to raise money for Reclaim the Night. Two burly men, who Diann believes were police, muscled their way into the fundraiser. In 2008, it was revealed that MacNeil had been on an RCMP watch list of left-wing subversives.

The largest and longest Reclaim the Night, according to *Groups Dynamic*, visited the lobby of the police station to express women's frustrations with the way the cops dealt with assault-and-battery cases.

If there was a march in the 1980s, Darl Wood was there.

"We liked to call ourselves professional activists," says Darl. "Rent-a-Dyke."

Darl remembers one Reclaim the Night when a group of "dykes" dealt with a jeering man by physically surrounding him. The fear Darl felt was not about physical harm, but of being seen.

For Diann, the fear soon turned to a feeling of empowerment.

"There's simply the joy of organizing something and having a whole lot of people show up," she says. "That's empowering. Or else we wouldn't have done it again!" She laughs.

In 1984, Diane Guilbault was working at Bryony House, a Halifax shelter for women and children impacted by intimate partner violence, when she took six of the shelter's residents to the march, organized that year by the

Dalhousie Women's Centre. "What an uplifting moment for them to walk the streets boldly and shout out their anger," Diane writes.

AnitaLouise Martinez was one of those residents. The 1984 Reclaim the Night march was the first march AnitaLouise attended after moving to Nova Scotia to live with her fourth, and final, husband in 1983. AnitaLouise left her husband and moved into Bryony House, where she lived for six weeks before moving into second-stage housing in Dartmouth. AnitaLouise stayed involved with Bryony House—which exists to this day—as a volunteer, driving women to pick up their belongings and doing court support, and later as a staff person.

"Just moving into Bryony house will make you political," AnitaLouise tells me at Lynn Murphy's apartment in December 2018. Bryony House was, she exclaims, the "best thing that ever happened to me!"

That first Reclaim the Night was "probably the strongest feeling I had in my lifetime," she says. "And I had a lot of kids," she adds with a hearty laugh.

Born in small-town Ontario in 1939, AnitaLouise had what she calls "a bit of a rocky childhood." Bruised and battered from her home life, she often wore three and four layers of clothing to school to hide the damage. She took refuge in the home of a Chinese family who ran a restaurant in her small town of Fort Erie.

When she was fifteen years old, AnitaLouise's father—who just *loved* Hitler, she tells me—was convicted of attempted murder. The court ordered that AnitaLouise move to Toronto and live with her grandparents, a "lovely" Welsh couple who had moved there from Newfoundland. She was seventeen when she married her first husband, and he—and each of her husbands after that—was exactly like her father. "I thought I was the bad girl and deserved it—until I got to Bryony House," she says. Bryony House was her refuge, somewhere she actually got some R-E-S-P-E-C-T.

Reclaim the Night was "like being born again somehow," AnitaLouise says.

"My eyes must have been like this," she says, wide-eyed. "Because I'm lookin' all around at all these women, *together*, marching!" Living at Bryony House was the first time Anita was exposed to "REAL LIVE HAPPY LESBIANS!" who worked or volunteered at the shelter.

"I was straight, supposedly," she says. "Damn, I wish I had known there was another way!" Meeting lesbians was "neat," says Anita. "It's when

I realized that I was feeling something towards one of them that I went and got counselling. I was beside myself!"

"Oh my God, did you go for counselling?" Lynn exclaims.

"I did!" Anita says, laughing. "I have one daughter who is lesbian. I told [her] as long as you don't hug or kiss in front of us. Boy, have I come a long way!"

Meredith and her partner, Diane Guilbault, were among the first lesbian couples that Anita met via the shelter. The pair, who met at a women's music night, would stroll down Barrington Street holding hands, just to "see how people would react," Meredith tells me with a laugh.

Meredith began volunteering with Bryony House because they had supported her after she was raped. Meredith, who was assaulted hitchhiking from Prince Edward Island, was one of five victims/survivors whose cases were tried together in New Glasgow. It was a "major trial."

"I'm a firm believer of, 'this organization has helped you out, so now, you know, pay it forward'," Meredith says. The assault also prompted Meredith to learn, and eventually start teaching, self-defence. Meredith, who often taught Wen-Do alongside Carol Millett, had many lesbian students.

Darl calls organizing Reclaim the Night "quite an amazing experience."

"I think one problem is that younger feminists don't have the same wonderful experience of coming together for something new, and fighting for something that has never been fought for before—and the sense of, dare I say, sisterhood that came about through that."

▼

The early 1980s was a busy time to be a lesbian feminist in Halifax.

"When I left, I calculated that I have been part of founding more than fifteen different women's organizations," says Brenda Bryan.

"We had lots of dances. We had lots of marches. We did all of that great stuff," says Susan, who remembers attending three or four meetings a week. "It was such a wonderful, wonderful time to be young and healthy and alive and a dyke in Halifax."

"That's when my life began, really. At fifty!" AnitaLouise says of the early 1980s. "My life began at fifty."

At nearly eighty years old now, the four-foot-eleven AnitaLouise is a staple at 2SLGBTQIA+ gatherings in Halifax. She started bringing her camera to events in 1984 and her visual timeline of the 2SLGBTQIA+ and feminist communities contains thousands of snaps.

"There was so much fire; there was so much passion," says Naomi Lechinsky.

In 1982 the Government of Canada introduced the Charter of Rights and Freedoms, which barred discrimination based on sex and other grounds. And there was no shortage of feminist groups or organizations: Bryony House, the Canadian Abortion Rights League (CARAL), the Elizabeth Fry Society, Forrest House, Mothers United for Metro Shelter (MUMS), the Women's Alliance in Support of Prostitutes (WASP), Voice of Women, Women Against Violence Against Women (WAVAW), and Women's Health Education Network (WHEN). In 1985 Brenda Bryan and Beth Ann Lloyd also founded Nova Scotia's feminist newspaper, *Pandora*.

Diann saw the feminist movement as accepting of lesbians. "You have to stick your nose in and demand that your perspective be heard," she says, sitting across from me at her dining table in north end Dartmouth. She shares her home with her partner of twenty-five years, Joan, and when I leave she

At a Reclaim the Night march in the 1980s. Front row (l–r): Diane Guilbault and AnitaLouise Martinez; back row (l–r): Verona Singer and K Tetlock.
(ANITALOUISE MARTINEZ COLLECTION)

gives me a photo of the couple and their dog, which they sent out in that year's holiday cards.

"I think that they grew used to us and, and I think also you win people's respect for the amount of work you're willing to do."

▼

Each year, International Women's Day would be capped off with a women's-only dance, first at the YWCA and later at Veith House. At the 1984 International Women's Day dance, a twenty-three-year-old Andrea Currie spotted a woman—who would become one of the great loves of her life, she says—across the dance floor. She remembers moving slowly across the room, eventually sitting in a chair closer to where the woman was dancing, trying to get up her nerve. For the first time in her life, Andrea asked a woman—this woman—to dance, and the two danced for the rest of the night. Afterwards Andrea, her crush, and her crush's gay sister stayed up most of the night talking, waking up sprawled across her bed in her shared home on Maynard Street.

A very snowy International Women's Day in 1980. **(DIANN GRAHAM COLLECTION)**

157

For Diann and her friends, their lives revolved around "the activities that we were doing in the lesbian community." IWD and the dance marked the beginning of spring, and the "Wild Wimmin Don't Get the Blues: Atlantic Wimmin's Retreat," the summer.

Wild Wimmin—which Diann calls a sort of Mini-Michigan Womyn's Music Festival—was first held in June 1983. That first weekend saw thirty to fifty women travel from across the Maritimes to "a beautiful country place, relatively isolated, surrounded by mountains," according to a Wild Wimmin Don't Get the Blues handout, about nine miles outside of Tatamagouche, Nova Scotia.

A handout for that first retreat, found in Anne's archives, called the weekend "a time and place to get together, make connections, talk, listen, listen to music, sing, go to workshops," on subjects that included butch and femme culture, coming out, women's spirituality, and lesbians and tools.

It felt like a safe space, says Diann. At the 2004 Lesbian Memory Keepers workshop, which Diann helped plan, attendees laughed as they remembered a weekend with "lots of nudity." Campers were stationed at the bottom of the dirt road to dissuade curious or ill-intentioned locals from interrupting.

Wild Wimmin's was the first time Brenda Bryan had camped and she was "scared shitless." It was a nice way for the city lesbians and the rural lesbians to connect, she says. There were women from Prince Edward Island, New Brunswick, rural Nova Scotia, and amongst them a group of Acadian women.

"Maybe one of the most magical evenings that I remember from Nova Scotia was at one of those weekends," says Susan Holmes. "Somebody was playing a guitar and Kate was playing her fiddle and the moon was up and the air was sweet and there was a firefly that walked on Kate's fiddle along the strings, blinking as it went.

"It was so beautiful."

The weekend was a "wimmin-only event" and while girl children were welcome, according to the handout, boy children over the age of four were not.

Girl-children-only policies—which weren't exclusive to Wild Wimmin's— were disappointing, says Sandra Nimmo. When it came to some women's gatherings, she was told, "Oh, well, you can come to the party and bring your little girls, but don't bring your son." Raising a young family and going back to school—she graduated from MSVU with a public relations degree, and from Dalhousie University with social work undergraduate and master's degrees—also meant that Sandra didn't have much free time to head across the harbour to the club.

Nancy Brister says she was also ostracized for having a male child. "And yet how are we going to train men to be sensitive, if we're not allowed to bring them?" she asks.

Brenda remembers women in the community discussing the finer points of being a lesbian separatist versus being a radical lesbian feminist and so on.

"It's like you felt betrayed if a lesbian feminist all of a sudden had a male friend back then," says Naomi. "That aspect of feminism I don't, I can't agree with. I didn't agree back then either."

Having spaces where women could be themselves is very, very important, she says, but adds, "I think sometimes there was a rigidity, absolutely, and the more radical lesbian feminist you were, that rigidity was very evident."

Lynn Murphy remembers reading a lot of lesbian separatist materials, which she got from Red Herring Cooperative Books. "It's true that working with men wasn't always ideal. Still isn't always ideal," she says. "I was willing to do it, whereas there were lesbian feminists (and these were women that I really admired because I thought they were the real activists) doing separatist things. I admired them, but I didn't see myself as being one of them."

Lynn identified then, and identifies now, as bisexual. "And of course within GAE they knew that there was no such thing as bisexual," she says. Diane Guilbault says that bisexual women were "given a hard time, as they were seen as repudiating lesbians and choosing the benefits of heterosexual relationships when it suited them. Lesbians felt betrayed by the bisexual women."

"It wasn't very accepted by anybody," Lynn says with a chuckle.

In 1979 Lynn began dating Arthur, the man she would marry. Though she generally avoided separatist events, several women she knew invited her to attend a lecture by a separatist visiting from BC.

"I toddled up to this do, and the woman began by saying she was speaking only to lesbians, and that if you were involved with a man, or ever had been involved with a man, then you were not part of the audience that she was addressing," says Lynn. The speaker asked anyone for whom that applied to leave, so Lynn did.

The local women came out during the coffee break and told Lynn, "This is awful. You were invited and you should stay."

"I thought that even for separatism that she had done a very bad thing, not necessarily to me, but to the lesbian mothers," says Lynn.

It was that kind of dogmatism that led Andrea to eventually become disenchanted with the lesbian feminist community. It felt like "a whole other kind of conformity," she says, so Andrea purposefully got involved with a man, which, she says, "blew me out of that community." The relationship didn't last, but she doesn't regret that decision.

▼

Likely the most famous—and infamous—women-only event was the Michigan Womyn's Music Festival. Founded in 1976, the festival featured big names of women's music including Cris Williamson, Meg Christian, Holly Near, Sweet Honey in the Rock, Ferron, Heather Bishop, BETTY (of lesbian TV show *The L Word* theme song fame), and the Indigo Girls.

Women's music—music made by and for women, often about loving women—was the unofficial soundtrack of early '80s lesbian feminism.

"I stopped listening to any other music," says Naomi. "I just listened to women's music for so many years."

Much of that music flowed from Oakland-based women's record label Olivia, founded in 1973 by a collective that included musician Meg Christian. Released by Olivia in 1975, Cris Williamson's *The Changer and the Changed* remained one of the top-selling independent albums in the US until the early 1990s. The cover of that album features a smiling Cris, topless in a pair of overalls, posing in front of a desert mountain range.

An article in a 1980 issue of GAE newsletter *Have You Heard* summed up some women's feelings about the genre. "Lesbians: Will One More Village People Song Drive You to Drink? Have You Recovered Totally From Disco Fever?" The article pointed out that library–card holders could borrow seventy women's music titles from the Dartmouth Regional Library. Both Heather Bishop and Holly Near played Halifax in the early 1980s.

The *Any Wymmin Can...Halifax Womens' Community Songbook* featured the lyrics to labour standards "Solidarity Forever" and "Bread and Roses," Meg

Christian's "Ode to a Gym Teacher," Holly Near's "Mountain Song/Kentucky Woman," and Alix Dobkin's "A Woman's Love," "Typical Canadian Dyke," and "I'm Tired of Fuckers Fucking Me Over."

"The music that we live with is an important part of our identity. Strong and loving words help us all to be strong and loving women," wrote the women who produced the songbook in 1980.

At the bottom of each page were messages, such as "any woman can... be strong, be free, play, laugh, be a winner"; "any woman can...be a lesbian"; and "any woman can...remember our foremothers who made the world better for us."

In 1980 Diann Graham travelled to the Michigan Womyn's Music Festival with three carloads of women from Halifax. Naomi, who made the pilgrimage to Michigan three or four times, remembers travelling "caravan style" to the festival.

It was "the most thrilling thing," says Naomi of the festival, which drew thousands of women and lesbians. "You know, every fantasy of believing that things could change kind of could happen there," she says.

"You are too young to remember Michigan the way that Michigan was," Susan tells me. "It was a community of ten thousand women that was safe. We could hold hands, which you couldn't anywhere. We could go naked if we wanted to. We could make love in the woods."

A queer millennial, I first learned of the festival when the organizers stubbornly stood by their "womyn born womyn" policy, which excluded transgender women. In 1991 a trans woman was removed from the festival after she was outed as trans. The incident sparked a protest camp, Camp Trans, which ran off-and-on for twenty years. In 2013 trans lesbian Red Durkin launched a petition calling on performers to boycott the event. In response, the Indigo Girls announced that that year's performance would be their last, until the festival reversed their policy. The festival folded in 2015.

"Everything just has its natural life," Diann tells me. "One can be nostalgic but...."

"I noticed a change the last time I was there," says Naomi. "I really noticed a change and it kind of saddened me because inclusivity is very important."

▼

In 1983, Diane Guilbault remembers sitting down with a group of women who had all been on the scene for more than five years to discuss the "state of affairs" of lesbian feminist organizing in Halifax. It had been some time since they had seen a new face at their organizing meetings.

"I don't know if it was burnout or just tired of not feeling like anything changed," says Diane, who was involved in organizing three Reclaim the Nights/Take Back the Nights and three International Women's Day marches. "Politics were being watered down, more conservative ('professional') women were getting involved, and they were definitely not lesbian."

A back-to-the-land-er, Diane had moved to Nova Scotia from Ontario in 1978 in search of a farm to buy. Unable to find what she was looking for, she enrolled in the kinesiology program at Dalhousie University. Within her first week in Halifax, Diane was attending meetings of various women's groups, and though the "lesbian community was not very visible," she began to run into the same women.

It was "a very exciting year for a country girl," says Diane.

As the 1980s wore on, "we really believed political action was becoming a thing of the past," says Diane.

"The old guard was starting to settle into long-term relationships and moving to the country to buy their homes," she writes. They were also going to visit women living in the country who would host weekend events. Pictou County and Yarmouth, particularly, were hot spots because of the number of lesbians who lived in those areas. Pictou County is, to this day, home to "a vibrant, active" lesbian community, Diane says.

▼

Susan Holmes and Naomi Lechinsky were roommates when they started talking about creating what would eventually become the Halifax Women's Housing Co-op in 1980 or 1981. Soon, two more women, Jackie McMahon and Sara Avmaat, joined the conversion and "then we decided, 'Why don't we try this?' It was just, 'Let's see what we can do.'" says Naomi. "There was so much openness."

The women—all lesbians—were in their twenties and thirties, "none in high paying jobs" and two were single mothers, while the other two wanted children in their lives. Many landlords wouldn't rent to people with kids, says Susan.

At the time, the Canadian Mortgage and Housing Corporation (CMHC) had a co-op program "which provided opportunities for low-income people to, as a group, buy or build urban homes," according to *We Dreamed Another Way of Being*, the report from the 2004 Lesbian Memory Keepers workshop.

They started off looking for a seven-bedroom house with one big common area, in a safe part of town. When they couldn't find "one huge house," they decided that they would have to acquire multiple properties, and brought on two other women, Diann Graham and Brenda Bryan. Slowly, other women, including Carol Millet, joined the passion project and the women hired a lawyer (now Nova Scotia Court of Appeal Justice), Anne Derrick. Naomi recalls "hours and hours and hours" of meetings, many at Forrest House, trying to reach a consensus about the soon-to-be co-op's values and policies. Soon the women were spending so much time on the co-op that their work at Forrest House "died off, and it greatly impacted the centre," says Brenda.

The Canada Mortgage and Housing Corporation didn't like the idea of a co-op that didn't allow men, reverse discrimination and all that nonsense, but there were already religious co-ops in existence, so they didn't say anything, says Susan.

Once each woman decided who they wanted to live with, the pairs/groups set off to find "low-cost housing" that worked for them.

Brenda Bryan, who had decided to live with three other women, remembers "schlepping around for months" looking at something like fifty-four houses before they found a duplex on Robie Street. Over the course of three years, the Halifax Women's Housing Co-op bought four houses, on Fuller Terrace, Robie Street, and Creighton Street in north end Halifax, and on Windmill Road in Dartmouth.

"We put our whole hearts into it because it was so significant to have housing security," says Brenda. In large part, it was about having control over their own housing "at a time when lesbians were not yet protected under the Nova Scotia human rights legislation." It was about creating a safe space, says Naomi.

"The Women's Housing Co-op came from people's actual experiences or fears of being denied housing," says Diann. "We weren't too far past [the time when] you had to have either your father or your husband's name on a bank loan to get a house."

It was also an opportunity for the young lesbians to create a family to "sort of make a home life for ourselves," says Diann—to celebrate birthdays and holidays together. "For us, to come out was to lose your family of origin, and if you weren't shunned, you were not embraced," continues Diann. "That meant young LG folk did not have their parents' resources to fall back on." Being rejected by your family and your church, "which was an important thing for people in the 1960s," was a terrible psychological blow, she adds.

When Susan and Carol went to take possession of the co-op's first house on Fuller Terrace, the people who had been renting it—Black folks from the North End—had yet to move out.

"I didn't know what we were going to do," says Susan, who was about to lose her own housing. She felt badly, and at that point it was "out of my hands. If I had walked away and not lived there, somebody else from the co-op was going to move in." Only later did the women learn that other co-ops approached similar situations by asking the former tenants to join the co-op.

"I needed my eyes opened a little bit more than they were then," Susan says. "It is what it is, but I can't pretend it didn't happen."

The property on Creighton Street had six very small units. Naomi used her carpentry skills to tear the house down to its beams, put up new drywall, and lay new floors. The women all "muddled along" and helped each other with renovations, she says.

They were young, says Diann, and weren't afraid of "Oh, you're going to have to drywall a whole house" or "You're going to have to stand on ladders and paint it all." The co-op was like "getting a PhD in things that usually men learned a lot about"—like mortgages and finances and renovations and repairs.

"The big mistake we made is that we moved in before we had it totally renovated," says Brenda of the Robie Street location. "We almost broke up a number of times because it was so stressful to try and do the repairs and live there at the same time." The end result, though, was beautiful.

Moving into the Creighton Street property was "was wonderful," says Naomi. "I had my own home," she says. "I had been on my own for a number of years and travelling around all over the place, so what I owned was a backpack and a sleeping bag. So having my own home—that was pretty nice." Her two-bedroom apartment included DIY wood floors, baseboards, and "fancy" trim, and was filled with lots of light and lots of plants.

When Susan and her daughter moved into the top unit in the house on Fuller Terrace, they moved into a working-class neighbourhood, home to members of various lefty and Communist groups, members of Four the Moment, people who worked at the Community Health Centre on Gottingen Street, and a number of gays, lesbians, and bisexuals. Even Lynn Murphy lived around the corner! Down the street was a condemned rooming house, soon to become a park, and two backyards away was the home of the local Hells Angels (although the co-op women only ever had to make one noise complaint). That first year at Christmas, Susan and her daughter went door-to-door carolling with a couple of friends. The next year, Carol and Susan organized a community carolling event in the park down the street, complete with camp-stove cider and tree decorating.

"It was a massive responsibility—over a million dollars worth of housing that we were controlling through feminist collective consensus decision making," Diann says with a laugh.

The co-op met at the beginning of every week and "we frequently had very uproarious meetings," she says. "There were vast disagreements."

Partners broke up and the co-op had to decide who stayed and who went. One member was going through a hard time and wasn't able to pay her rent, and they had to discuss eviction. There were debates about whether boy children would be allowed and what would happen when they grew into men. It was co-op policy to take two meetings to make any decision, allowing members to step away and revisit the issue, perhaps with cooler heads. Six of the women even took a course in conflict resolution, says Brenda.

"The meetings, emotionally, were very draining," says Susan, who's daughter Karen also attended. During one meeting, where the women were discussing allocation of funds for repairs, Karen drew a picture of the house on Creighton Street. In each window she drew a crying face, bags of money soaring through the air. Susan imagines some of her daughter's drawings are still in the co-op's minutes.

The co-op was made of "really great minds" who were able to approach their challenges from a variety of perspectives, says Susan. On one occasion when the co-op was having trouble, rather than hiring a mediator, Brenda suggested bringing in an improv dance teacher to work with the group—and it worked.

"We were young," says Naomi, who was twenty when she came to Halifax. "We were naive on some levels and emotionally maybe not as mature as we are now, but I think that our hearts and our minds were in a really, really good place."

Everybody was committed to the higher good, says Carol, who wrote about the housing co-op for *Groups Dynamic*. "I was going to call the article 'The Joys of Owning a House—With Twelve Others!' Catchy, eh?" she joked. "But I can hear the gasps of disbelief now. How can owning anything, let alone a bunch of houses, be joyful?" For Carol, much of that joy came from a seemingly unlikely source: the co-op's meetings. "They weren't a chore for me," she tells me during our interview. "I looked forward to going to those meetings." The joy, Carol wrote in *Groups Dynamic*, came when the women were "consensed" on a decision. Consensus "creates such a solid, solid foundation for a community," she says.

It was a time of really "living our politics in an honest way," says Brenda.

The United Spinsters affinity group held meetings at the house, says Diann, and the co-op women joked that the phones were bugged because they could hear a click, click, click, click. Their suspicions seemed to be confirmed, though, when one of the co-op members picked up the phone and could hear someone on the other end. "Oh, our lines must be crossed," said the voice. It was a janitor at the Stadacona military base, trying to call his wife.

"I remember that most of us had our phones tapped," says Susan. "I had my mail opened occasionally."

Susan was a single mother living on unemployment insurance in 1981 or 1982 when she fell ill. She later realized that one of the causes of her health problems was her one hundred-year-old co-op house; more precisely, the mould. In 1984 Susan—now working in student services and admissions at NSCAD—realized she was working "way beyond" her limits and began attending, as opposed to organizing, events. Susan moved out of her co-op house and into an apartment in 1987, and that's when she got really sick, with what she now knows are severe environmental sensitivities. Her illness prevents her from visiting Nova Scotia, but when I sent her a recent *Halifax Magazine* article on the co-op she was pleased to know that it has survived and kept its principles.

"It was home and we built it. We made it," says Susan. "That's a very powerful feeling and I'm really glad that there are women still living in it—dykes, I hope," she says with a laugh.

Similarly, Diann judges the co-op's success on that fact that it is still going all these years later, and that it is providing housing for women in need. "I know that there was a lot of conflict and I know that there was a lot of hardship and hurt and angst. But looking at it, I just feel a tremendous sense of accomplishment.

"Is it a feminist lesbian utopia? Noooo. But is it a reasonable facsimile of the dream of eight women, all in their twenties, who said, 'Let's make a co-op and live together?' It's a big success," says Diann.

"I sometimes reflect on that time as very insular," says Naomi, who was working as a cobbler at the time. "It was a very strong, dynamic group that I hung out with and we did everything together. We lived together; we organized together."

Three decades later, many of the original co-op members are still in touch. In fall 2018, when Naomi visited the east coast, Diann threw her a party, inviting women she hadn't seen in years. It was beautiful, says Naomi. "There was such a willingness and an open-heartedness to just really care about each other and support each other," Naomi says of her former housemates. "I will always love those women, that's the only way I can say it," she says, tearing up in her office in Toronto. "They were like my family. And I learned a lot and I'm grateful—and as you can see, it moves me. It was powerful."

Chapter 8

LGB LEGACY: PRESERVING OUR PAST

When I first interviewed Nancy Brister in 2016, for the Coast *article "Before the* Parade," she was still getting used to being called an elder. When we reconnected two years later for this book, I asked her if that was still the case.

"Well you see, it's a shock, you know," she responds. "Because you still live in your memories. And in my memories I'm not an elder."

This book, I've been told a number of times, has gotten a lot of LGB2S elders revisiting those memories, solo, with me, and together. In addition to the who, what, where, and when, it's also got people thinking about how what they did "back then" has shaped our community, our world today.

Researching this book, I interviewed around thirty gay, lesbian, bisexual, queer, and two-spirit elders. As Robin Metcalfe told me early on in our friendship (and it's something I often repeat), a generation is not a monolith. So when I asked people what they thought their generation's legacy was, it was no surprise that I got a wide variety of answers.

GAE's legacy, Deborah Trask told me was: "The fact that you're even interested."

She also directed me to The Turret, and Rumours after that. "That there was a gay community centre in downtown Halifax, run by the community at a time where there was no such other place anywhere in the country," she says. "It didn't survive, but the effects are still being felt."

I was with Deborah at her home on Nova Scotia's South Shore the day I found out about the Pulse Orlando shooting. The night before, a gunman had killed forty-nine people at the gay bar's Latin night. The details were still sparse that morning and I was in shock. I had not yet tapped into the planning for the next day's vigil. After our interview, Deborah sent me home with her original Turret T-shirt and an arm full of Janis Joplin vinyl.

The next day I received an email from Lynn Murphy, sparked by something Pulse's owner had said about why they opened the club: to create a space for the community to meet and dance. "Surely that's a simple enough desire, to dance in safety?" she wrote, noting how little attention was paid to the fact that the victims and survivors were primarily Latinx and Black.

It had her thinking about the importance of her generation's safe space, The Turret. "The Turret club (and later Rumours) was a safe space for LGBT people to meet," she wrote. "We built and enhanced our social networks. In our own space we discussed internal issues—politics of drag, LGBT parenting, violence within LGBT relationships. We created our own artistic expressions. We began to see ourselves as a people with common goals, not just as 'queer' individuals."

She signed off: "I hope you are doing OK."

We may not currently have a Turret, or an official community centre in which to gather, but these types of interactions instill in me a definite sense of "we're in this together"-ness that spans generations.

"People should know that it could and can be again," Chris Shepherd says of his beloved Turret and the community it fostered.

And people—young gay, lesbian, bisexual, and two-spirit folks—got their footing: the Annes, the Robins, the Mary Anns, the Deborahs, the Jims, the Lornes, the Lynns, the Chrises, the Randys, the Dianns, the Darls, the Andreas, and more.

"There was a Help Line that people could call and ask questions and reach out for help," says Katherine MacNeil. "There were some people who were not afraid to put themselves out there as role models or mentors for anyone who needed that."

"I told myself at the beginning I wanted to make things easier for those who came behind," Deborah Trask said when she spoke on the Pride Nova Scotia panel at Government House in 2018, the Pride flag blowing in the wind out front. "There were hundreds of us trying in our own small ways, and looking back, I think we did make a difference."

▼

"Maybe Pride is our legacy?" Katherine tells me on the back deck of her home, nestled alongside the Mira River, not far from where I spent my summers growing up.

Katherine recalls a recent Cape Breton Pride parade in Sydney, which I, my girlfriend, her sister, and her sister's wife also attended. The passing floats were playing some of the music they used to spin at The Turret. Katherine turned to a young person beside her, decked out in rainbow attire, and said, "You know, that music was in style forty-plus years ago." They sort of just looked at Katherine and laughed. They probably couldn't imagine forty-plus years ago, Katherine tells me.

"Maybe when they see an old grey-haired woman...they don't think of me as being one of them," she tells me. "But it was very comfortable, everybody was comfortable. In part, that must be our legacy."

Many people I spoke to were at the first Pride march in Halifax in 1988.

Jim MacSwain explains that the Pride marches of the late 1980s were, in part, a way to "tell people that we were still here" during the height of the AIDS crisis in North America. The "positive nature" of the march-turned-parade, Jim says, was a way to counter the media narrative that "everybody was dying" of AIDS.

"There was a sense of daring and there was a sense of making a statement," says Darl Wood, who marched in her first Pride in Toronto in the early 1980s. "It was a celebration for sure, but it wasn't just a celebration, it was a political statement."

Darl doesn't attend Pride parades much any more. "One I went to, they had all of these floats and then at the end of the parade were the lesbians and gays walking," she says. "To me they are the prime reason for the parade. The other things can go, that's fine, but you don't discount the people. I think that's what's lost today."

"I value what we did it because I think it did have an impact," says Naomi Lechinsky. "Sometimes I wonder how far we've gone back."

I was at the Nova Scotia Archives in May 2019—combing through microfilm copies of business directories from the 1960s and 1970s—when I received a call from AnitaLouise Martinez. "Rebecca, are you in Halifax?" she asked me in an urgent tone. I was, I told her. "You *must* come over." Anita's friend, Meredith Bell, was in town, staying with her, and they had been talking about their shared history.

Politics in general, Meredith told me with a deep sigh, have just gone so haywire—so backwards. "It is like starting over again because people have lost, sort of, the connections and access to the references or the resources," says Meredith. "Which is sad."

The history, Meredith says, "should be out there, because we find ourselves starting over again, which I think is absolutely ridiculous."

"We believed that we could change the world, and we did," says Darl. "That generation really did change the world."

▼

When GALA (the Gay and Lesbian Association of Nova Scotia, a later version of GAE) and the second Rumours folded in 1995, Lynn Murphy acted quickly to salvage what she could of the organization. She said, "Oh my God, we've got to get the papers out."

A former librarian and self-described archives keener, she tucked the files away in a safe and undisclosed location: her basement. When she downsized to an apartment, Lynn donated the boxes to the Nova Scotia Archives.

During our first interview in 2016, Lynn told me that she has not looked at the files since.

"Well, I have," I say.

"You have?!" she exclaimed with glee.

There was a time, Robin Metcalfe says, when he and his peers knew that they were "getting older" and didn't know any younger 2SLGBTQIA+ folks who seemed keen on taking on the archives, as they were.

"Who are we going to give this stuff to?" he remembers thinking.

"The latest generation of activists has given me hope that there are successors, there are people to whom I may be able to pass things on," Robin told me in 2016, "whether it be information, knowledge, actual objects, or archives."

About a decade ago, when I was on the Board of the Nova Scotia Rainbow Action Project (NSRAP), Chris Aucoin loaned me a copy of the beautifully titled *We Dreamed Another Way of Being*. This was long before I was writing about Nova Scotian 2SLGBTQIA+ history, and so once I read it, I made a copy (like the good little archivist that I am) and filed it in my chest with the rest of my queer and trans archival materials. That document, and the *Groups Dynamic* booklet, has been invaluable to my research and writing.

In 2019, when I sat down to talk to Diann Graham for this book, I learned how *We Dreamed Another Way* came to be. In 2003, Diann retired from her job at Women's Employment Outreach, where she had worked for twenty-two years, and had some time on her hands.

Reflecting on her time in Halifax, all that she and her peers had accomplished, and everything that had changed, Diann reached out to a handful of women to figure out just how they could honour and document that herstory. A former history student, Diann knew how "invisible women are in history."

The Lesbian Memory Keepers workshop itself was a collective effort, and about forty-five women came together at the Universalist Unitarian Church, despite a quintessential Nova Scotia snowstorm. Several "young lesbians" in their forties took notes.

"The day was wonderful and glorious, and we sang, and we told stories, and we laughed uproariously, and it was like, 'Remember when and remember when?'" says Diann.

The day their final report was accepted into the Nova Scotia Archives, the committee members all attended the signing of the paperwork, and then went for a drink. There was such a feeling of accomplishment, says Diann.

"You have it, lots of people have it, so the voices [will] never be lost. What we accomplished [will] never be lost," she says.

There has been much discussion amongst the people I have talked to for this book about where to store their personal collections. There is the Canadian Lesbian and Gay Archives in Toronto—originally an offshoot of *The Body Politic*—but up until now there has been nothing of the sort in Nova Scotia. The Nova Scotia Archives boasts the most substantial public collection of our community's historical documents, but it is not explicitly 2SLGBTQIA+.

While writing this book, a group of people started meeting to discuss the possibility of creating a queer and trans archive in Nova Scotia. In 2019,

Jacqueline Gahagan—a researcher at Dalhousie University—received funding from the Nova Scotia Department of Seniors to create a province-wide digital 2SLGBTQIA+ "Seniors Archive." That project led to discussions between members of the Atlantic History and Archives network—a group of community members "interested in preserving our history by routing important documents to permanent locations where they'll be kept in safe conditions and made available to future researchers and community members"—about establishing a physical 2SLGBTQIA+ home at the Dalhousie Archives.

▼

I am sitting on the floor at Robin Metcalfe's apartment; both of our iPhones sit beside me, recording. It is May 2019 and we're listening to a 1983 conversation between a young Robin, Anne Fulton, and Diane Warren. As the warmth from a few whiskies reaches my cheeks, the voices of Anne and Diane, two lesbian elders, founding members of the first LGB advocacy group in Nova Scotia, whom I've never met, wash over me. We've got the volume up high so that we can decipher the tape, recorded the year before I was born. You can hear the clink of the teapot, the cups, the spoons stirring milk and sugar.

Midway through the recording, Anne announces that her "coming out anniversary" is on the horizon. It will be twelve years. "I've been out for ten years this year," Robin chimes in. "You're catching up to me!" Anne exclaims with a chuckle. "I'm sixteen in May," adds Diane.

The tape was only one of many that Robin recent recently re-discovered in four binders of cassette tapes of recordings of GAE interviews, news items, or call-in shows centred on homosexuality, and interviews with key LGB figures in the province. I would like to have listened to and transcribed every single one of those tapes before I finished this book, but there simply was not time.

On the morning of May 10, 2019, I woke up surrounded by the hills of Mabou, Cape Breton. I was there to interview Andrea Currie. The first draft of my manuscript was due in June, but in the highlands of Cape Breton it didn't look like June was coming anytime soon. But it was, which meant my interview with Andrea would be one of my last.

While writing this book I have kept a spreadsheet simply entitled "people," of 2SLGBTQ people whom I would like to either interview or include in the book in some way. As of this writing, there are approximately eighty people on this list.

As Andrea Currie pointed out to me in our interview, really, my research followed the "path of relationships." My list started small, and grew each time I spoke to someone new, and they put me in touch with a friend or an ex-lover.

In our interview, Andrea poetically described her own life as "a bouquet." And that's how I think about this history—as a bouquet, a collection, of people, of stories. As my research progressed, I added more and more flowers.

There are so many more people that I want to talk to, but given my parameters, it was simply impossible to talk to everyone—another reason this book is "A" and not "The" history of gay, lesbian, and bisexual Halifax. I know that when this book is released into the world, it will bring forth an untold number of stories that I wasn't able to capture here. I look forward to hearing those stories, and to meeting the people who share them.

I know that this is not the last I will be writing about our 2SLGBTQIA+ histories; I have a feeling that this will be my life's work, and I am okay with that.

The bouquet can only get more full, more unruly, more tangled, more beautiful.

A NOTE ON SOURCES

This book draws upon hundreds of historical documents from the Gay and Lesbian Association of Nova Scotia fonds in the Nova Scotia Archives. I also relied heavily on back issues of the *Dalhousie Gazette*, available online through the Dalhousie University Archives, and on back issues of *The Body Politic* that were available online though the Canadian Museum for Human Rights.

I was kindly given access to the personal archives of Diann Graham, Jim MacSwain, Robin Metcalfe, Sandra Nimmo, Anthony Trask, and Deborah Trask, and those of Anne Fulton by way of Robin Metcalfe. Thank you to Anne Fulton's family for giving me permission to use and quote from those materials.

I regularly referenced the GayHalifax wiki, created and maintained by Dan MacKay, and I am particularly grateful for Reg Giles's "Peanut Butter And Jam Sandwich (Thru My Eyes)" and Scott MacNeil's "Reflections in a Mirror Ball," which are both hosted on the site.

The lesbian and feminist history contained within this book is largely drawn from the pages of *Groups Dynamic: A Collection of Nova Scotia Her-Stories*, published by the Canadian Congress for Learning Opportunities for Women in 1990, and from *We Dreamed of Another Way of Being: Report of the Lesbian Memory Keepers Workshop*.

I conducted in-person or phone interviews with Frank Abbott, Meredith Bell, Walter Borden, Nancy Brister, Brenda Bryan, Tom Burns, Andrea Currie, Reg Giles, Diann Graham, Susan Holmes, Lorne Izzard, Randy Kennedy, Naomi Lechinsky, Katherine MacNeil, Jim MacSwain, AnitaLouise Martinez, Robin Metcalfe, Carol Millett, Lynn Murphy, Sandra Nimmo, Faith Nolan, Mike Sangster, Chris Shepherd, Anthony Trask, Deborah Trask, and Darl Wood. I did email interviews with Diane Guilbault and Barbara James. Access to an interview with Mary Ann Mancini was kindly granted by Allie Jaynes.

ACKNOWLEDGEMENTS

I'd like to offer my thanks to the following people (and places).

The two-spirit, lesbian, bisexual, gay, queer, transgender, genderqueer, and gender-nonconforming elders who made it possible for me to exist, survive, thrive, and resist, in Nova Scotia and beyond. Each and every person who trusted me with their stories, let me root through old boxes, put me in touch with friends, and answered my many phone calls, emails, and Facebook messages. I will not list you all here; your names are woven through these pages.

My mother for, well, everything. But especially for imbuing in me the importance of family, community, heritage, and history. My father for his curiosity, long discussions, and for passing down that writing gene. My little sister for being the strongest ally from an impossibly young age, and for making me laugh so darn hard. To the three of you for loving me—and teaching me to love—so fiercely.

My Jill. I couldn't have dreamt up a more (enthusiastically) supportive, understanding, loving, beautiful, and brilliant partner. Thank you for building this little life with me. May we continue to push each other to do and be our best. I love you.

My entire extended family—The Dillons, Roses, MacAulays, and Marshes—for teaching me the importance of family and for the love and support even when you didn't understand. To Jill's family—the Staggs—for welcoming me, and for your unwavering care and support.

Round Island—my favourite place on earth, and my first taste of community.

My fellow student movement and queer and trans peers who have made the impossible (feel) possible.

My friends—my chosen family—some of whom I've known since childhood, some since high school, others from university, and still others from my time in San Francisco. A special thank you to Liz for transcribing an interview when I was in the thick of it.

Jacob Boon for believing in writing about Halifax's radical histories, for the copious edits, and for being the first person who said this should be a book. To *The Coast* for publishing the article "Before The Parade," which started this whole journey, and for allowing me to use that title for this book. To everyone who has hired—and paid—this radical, queer, feminist writer.

To Chris Aucoin for giving us permission to base the cover on his fantastic design.

To the staff at the Nova Scotia Archives for your direction and encouragement.

To Whitney Moran at Nimbus: this wouldn't be a book if you hadn't seen something book-worthy in that article, and in me. Thanks for understanding that the history of this province includes queer and trans history. To my editor, Angela Mombourquette: thank you for being even more "thorough" than me, and for working so hard to get the book to where it is today.

To Leslie Feinberg for *Stone Butch Blues*, the first book in which I saw our history and my queer femme identity reflected. To the queer and trans historians and writers whose work I am building upon.

BIBLIOGRAPHY

Agger, Ellen. "Lesbians Fight to Keep Kids." *The Body Politic*, December 1976/ January 1977.

Birch-Bayley, Nicole. "A Vision Outside the System: A Conversation with Faith Nolan about Social Activism and Black Music in Contemporary Canada." *Postcolonial Text*, Vol. 6, No. 3, 2011. Laurentian University.

Broverman, Neal. "'Patient Zero': Correcting the Record on a Media-Made Gay Villain." *The Advocate*, May 14, 2018.

CATIE: Canada's Source for HIV and Hepatitis C Information. "A History of HIV/AIDS." catie.ca/en/world-aids-day/history.

"Conference '78: Making It Strong." *The Body Politic*, June/July 1978.

DeYoung, Jim. "Interview with Bill Pusztai." GayHalifax Wiki, 2011. gay.hfxns.org/JimDeYoung.

Doctor Barry's Royal Commission on the Non-Medical Use of Love, Sex, and Politics, Vol. 1, No. 0 (October 17, 1982).

Dose, Ralf. *Magnus Hirschfeld: The Origins of the Gay Liberation Movement*. New York: Monthly Review Press, 2014.

"Editorial." *The Sisters' Lightship*, Vol. 1, No. 1 (December 1978).

Fulton, Anne. "Gayline Report." February 14, 1983.

Fulton, Anne. "Jury Room—Guilty." *The Voice*, September, 1977.

Fulton, Anne. "The Lesbian Conference: We Recognize the Need." *The Voice,* July, 1976.

GAE. "A Brief Regarding the Human Rights Act." March 5, 1973.

———. "GAE Plans Censorship Protest [Press Release]." January 23, 1979.

———. *GAE/Y Information Service.* Vol. 1, No. 3 (May 24, 1973).

———. General Meeting Minutes. Various dates.

———. *Have You Heard?* Vol. 2, No. 5 (November 23, 1979).

———. "Letter to and Survey of Candidates in April 2 Provincial Election." March 9, 1974.

———. "Letter to CBC Radio Studios." January 9, 1976.

———. "Letter to Mr. Arthur Ward, City of Halifax (Legal Reform Committee)." 1974.

———. "Letter to Mr. F. W. Pace, Director of Recruitment and Selection, Civil Service Commission (Legal Reform Committee)." April 3, 1974.

"GAE Protests." *Dalhousie Gazette,* January 25, 1979.

———. "Report of the Conference Planning Committee." August 2, 1978.

———. "Results of its Poll of Candidates in the April 2nd Provincial Election on their Stand on Gay Rights [Press Release]." March 30, 1974.

———. "Statement to the News Media [Press Release]." March 5, 1973.

———. *The Voice,* No. 1 (July 1976).

———. *The Voice,* No. 2 (April 1977).

"Gaetan Dugas." GayHalifax Wiki. http://gay.hfxns.org/GaetanDugas.

Garmaise, David and Michael Lynch. "Gays in Six Cities Protest: CBC Bans Public Service Ads." *The Body Politic,* March 1977.

"Gazette Boycotts CBC Ads." *Dalhousie Gazette,* December 9, 1976.

Giles, Reg. "Peanut Butter And Jam Sandwich (Thru My Eyes)." GayHalifax Wiki. gay.hfxns.org/PeanutButterAndJamSandwichIndex.

Gleason, Tim. "Anti Gayzette." *The Dalhousie Gazette,* February 10, 1977.

"Group Denied Media Access." *4th Estate,* May 12, 1976.

Groups Dynamic: A Collection of Nova Scotia Her-Stories. Canadian Congress for Learning Opportunities for Women, 1990.

"Halifax Women are Reclaiming the Night." *Dalhousie Gazette,* October 5, 1978.

Hooper, Thomas Harold. *"Enough is Enough": The Right to Privacy Committee and Bathhouse Raids in Toronto, 1978–83."* (December 2016). York University.

Hooper, Tom. "Canada is Releasing a Coin Commemorating a Myth: That Homosexuality was Decriminalized in 1969." CBC Opinions, April 22, 2019.

Hooper, Tom, Gary Kinsman, Karen Pearlston. "Anti-69 FAQ." ActiveHistory. ca. Accessed March 14, 2019. anti-69.ca/faq.

Jackson, Ed. "Mayor Drags Feet on Cop/Gay Study." *The Body Politic,* July/August 1981.

Jackson, Ed. "The Night They Raided Truxx." *The Body Politic,* August 1978.

Jaynes, Allie. Interview with Mary Ann Mancini. September 23, 2014.

Jones, Burnley "Rocky" and James W. St.G. Walker. *Burnley "Rocky" Jones: Revolutionary.* Black Point, NS: Roseway Publishing, 2016.

Kerans, Marion Douglas. *Muriel Duckworth: A Very Active Pacifist.* Black Point, NS: Fernwood Publishing, 1996.

Kinsman, Gary and Patrizia Gentile. *The Canadian War on Queers: National Security as Sexual Regulation.* Vancouver: UBC Press, 2009.

Kinsman, Gary William and Patrizia Gentile. *We Still Demand! Redefining Resistance in Sex and Gender Struggles*. Vancouver: UBC Press, 2016.

Korinek, Valerie Joyce. *Prairie Fairies*. Toronto: University of Toronto Press, 2018.

Landry-Milton, Marci. "Gay Lib comes to Halifax; GAE Gives 'Liberation Through Pride.'" *Dalhousie Gazette*, February 2, 1973.

Lewis, Bill and Randy Coates. "Moral Lessons; Fatal Cancer." *The Body Politic*, October 1981.

MacNeil, Kathy. "Eets Meets." *The Body Politic*, June/July 1978.

MacNeil, Scott. "Reflections in a Mirror Ball." GayHalifax Wiki. gay.hfxns. org/ReflectionsInAMirrorBall.

Mansour, V. and H. MacKinnon. "CBC: Coast to Coast—Almost." *Dalhousie Gazette*, January 6, 1977.

McLeod, Donald W. *Lesbian and Gay Liberation in Canada: A Selected Annotated Chronology 1964-1975*. Toronto: Homewood Books, 1996.

McLeod, Donald W. *Lesbian and Gay Liberation in Canada: A Selected Annotated Chronology, 1976-1981*. Toronto: Homewood Books, 2016.

Metcalfe Robin. "Bar Expels Gays, GAE Pickets, Calls for Boycott." *The Body Politic*, July/August 1977.

———. "CBC Bureaucrat Imposes Ban on Gay Ads." *The Body Politic*, October 1976.

———. "Customs Blocks Lesbian Books." *The Body Politic*, November 1978.

———. "Demo Protests State Censors." *The Body Politic*, March/April 1979.

———. "Gays and the Canadian Law." *Dalhousie Gazette, Gay Supplement*, September 23, 1976.

———. "Gay People vs. CBC." *The Voice*, April 1977.

———. "Halifax: Movement Aids Gay Community Development." *The Body Politic*, April 1976.

———. "Liberation through Education." *The Body Politic*, December 1975.

Millet, Carol. *The GAE Presents Illicit Politics and Subversive Sex*. October 1983.

Murphy, Lynn. "Living Gay: 4th Atlantic Conference in Fredericton." *Making Waves*, July 1982.

Nepean, Greg. "Towards An Experience Of Gay History." GayHalifax Wiki. gay.hfxns.org/TowardsAnExperienceOfGayHistory.

NGRC. "CBC Bans Gay Announcements." *The Body Politic*, June 1976.

NGRC Forum. *News-and-Views Bulletin of the National Gay Rights Coalition*. Summer 1976.

Nolan, Faith. "A Whole Other Story," in *Any Other Way: How Toronto Got Queer*, eds. John Lorinc et al. Toronto: Coach House Books, 2017.

Raj, Rupert. "Worlds in Collision," in *Any Other Way: How Toronto Got Queer*, eds. John Lorinc et al. Toronto: Coach House Books, 2017.

Reynolds, Daniel. "Patricia Nell Warren, The Front Runner Author, Dies at 82." *The Advocate*, February 10, 2019.

Rose, Rebecca. "Before the Parade." *The Coast (Halifax)*, July 21, 2016.

Ross, Becki L. *The House That Jill Built: A Lesbian Nation in Formation*. Toronto: University of Toronto Press, 1995.

S., Bill. "Woman's Day at Rumors." *GAE presents THE NEWS and….* May 1983.

Stout, Bob. "GAE and the Halifax Media." *The Voice*, July, 1976.

Taormino, Tristan. "Trouble in Utopia." *Village Voice*, September 12, 2000.

"The Gazette Responds." *Dalhousie Gazette,* February 10, 1977.

Trainor, Carole, ed. *And I Will Paint the Sky: Women Speak the Story of Their Lives.* Lawrencetown Beach: Pottersfield Press, 2001.

Tucker, Karen Iris. "Is It Wrong to Perform at Michfest?" *The Advocate,* May 28, 2013.

Union of Nova Scotia Indians, The Confederacy of Mainland Mi'kmaq, and the Native Council of Nova Scotia. "Contemporary Mi'kmaq – Kiskukewaq Mi'kmaq." In *Mi'kmaw Resource Guide.* Truro, NS: Eastern Woodland Publishing, 2007.

Warren, Diane, entry. GayHalifax Wiki. gay.hfxns.org/DianeWarren.

"We Dreamed of Another Way of Being: Report of the Lesbian Memory Keepers Workshop." November 13, 2004.

Zdunich, Allan. "Policy or Local Prejudice." *Dalhousie Gazette, Gay Supplement,* September, 23, 1976.

LINDSAY DUNCAN

Rebecca Rose is a Cape Breton–born queer femme, feminist, and freelance writer who has spent her adult life going between Halifax and Toronto. She currently lives in Dartmouth, NS, with her partner and her cat. Rebecca's writing focuses on queer and trans people, communities, and histories; misogyny and feminism; and social movements. She has a journalism degree from Ryerson University. Rebecca's own queer activism has spanned the last decade, including involvement in Nova Scotia's 2SLGBTQIA+ advocacy group and as a founding member of the Halifax Dyke and Trans March.